Masters of Wisdom of Central Asia

Masters of Wisdom of Central Asia

Teachings from the Sufi Path of Liberation

Hasan Lutfi Shushud

Translated from the Turkish by Muhtar Holland

Inner Traditions
Rochester, Vermont • Toronto, Canada

Inner Traditions
One Park Street
Rochester, Vermont 05767
www.InnerTraditions.com

SUSTAINABLE FORESTRY INITIATIVE Certified Sourcing www.sfiprogram.org SFI-00854
Text stock is SFI certified

Originally published in Turkish in 1958 by Doğan Kardeş Yayinlri A. Ş. Basimevi under the title *Hâcegân Hânedâni*
First English edition published in the United Kingdom in 1983 by Coombe Springs Press under the title *Masters of Wisdom of Central Asia*
Revised second edition published in 2014 by Inner Traditions

Library of Congress Cataloging-in-Publication Data

Shushud, Hasan Lutfi.
[Islâm tasavvufunda hâcegân hânedâni. English]
Masters of wisdom of Central Asia : Sufi teachings of the Naqshbandi lineage / Hasan Lutfi Shushud. — Second edition.
pages cm
Includes bibliographical references.
ISBN 978-1-62055-361-9 (paperback) — ISBN 978-1-62055-362-6 (e-book)
1. Naqshabandiyah—Asia, Central—History. 2. Naqshabandiyah—Turkey—History. 3. Naqshabandiyah—Doctrines. I. Title.
BP189.7.N35S5413 2014
297.4'1—dc23

2014015125

Printed and bound in the United States by Lake Book Manufacturing, Inc.
The text stock is SFI certified. The Sustainable Forestry Initiative® program promotes sustainable forest management.

10 9 8 7 6 5 4 3 2 1

Text design by Virginia Scott Bowman and layout by Priscilla Baker
This book was typeset in Times New Roman, with Garamond Premier Pro, Legacy Serif, and Cambria used as display typefaces

Contents

Foreword by Nevit Ergin ix

About the Author—An Autobiographical Note xi

Introduction 1

The Importance of Khwāja Yūsuf al-Hamadānī 7

Three of the Deputies of Khwāja Yūsuf al-Hamadānī 12

Khwāja ʻAbdallāh Barqī 12

Khwāja Ḥasan al-Andāqī 12

Khwāja Aḥmad al-Yasavī, "Top Link" for the Turkish Shaikhs 14

The Chain of Transmission of the Yasaviyya
Through the Four Deputies of Khwāja Aḥmad al-Yasavī 20

Manṣūr Ata and His Family Lineage 21

Sa'īd Ata of Khwārizm 21

Sulaymān Ata, Great Turkish Shaikh 21

Ḥakīm Ata 22

The Line of Transmission through Zengi Ata, Deputy of Ḥakīm Ata 23

The Deputies of Zengi Ata: Uzun Ḥasan Ata, Sayyid Ata, Ṣadr Ata, Badr Ata 24

The Deputies of Sayyid Ata 25

Ismāʻīl Ata 25

Isḥāq Khoja 25

Kamāl Shaikh Īkānī 26

Khadim Shaikh 27

Khwāja 'Abd al-Khāliq al-Ghujdawānī
Fourth Deputy of Khwāja Yūsuf al-Hamadānī 29
Khwāja 'Abd al-Khāliq's Letter of Counsel 30
The Principles of the Way of the Masters 31

The Deputies of Khwāja 'Abd al-Khāliq Ghujdawānī 35
Khwāja Aḥmad Ṣiddīq, First Deputy of Khwāja 'Abd al-Khāliq Ghujdawānī 35
Khwāja Awlīyā' Kabīr, Second Deputy of Khwāja 'Abd al-Khāliq Ghujdawānī 35
Khwāja Sulaymān Germīnī, Third Deputy of Khwāja 'Abd al-Khāliq Ghujdawānī 37
Khwāja 'Ārif Riwgarī, Fourth Deputy of Khwāja 'Abd al-Khāliq Ghujdawānī 37
Khwāja Maḥmūd Faghnawī, Successor of Khwāja 'Ārif Riwgarī 37

Khwāja 'Azīzān 'Alī al-Rāmitanī
One of the Greatest of the Masters of Wisdom 39
Khwāja Muḥammad Baba Sammāsī 42
Sayyid Amīr Kulāl 43

Khwāja Muḥammad Bahā' al-Dīn 'Shah' Naqshband and His Contemporaries 46
Khalīl Ata, Eminent Turkish Shaikh 50
Mawlānā Bahā' al-Dīn Qishlāqī and Mawlānā 'Ārif Dikkarānī 51
Pilgrimage and Passing of Khwāja Bahā' al-Dīn Naqshband 52
Sayings of the Venerable Khwāja Naqshband 54
Some Remarkable Episodes in the Life of Khwāja Naqshband 57

Seven of the Major Deputies of Khwāja Bahā' al-Dīn Naqshband 62
Khwāja Muḥammad Parsā 62
Khwāja Burhān al-Dīn Abū Naṣr-i Parsā 65
Khwāja Musāfir Khwārizmī 65
Mawlānā Muḥammad Figanzī 66
Mawlānā Ya'qūb Charkhī 67
Khwāja 'Alā' al-Dīn Ghujdawānī 68
Mawlānā Saif al-Dīn Mannārī 69
Shaikh Sirāj al-Dīn Kulāl Pīrmesī 69

Khwāja 'Alā' al-Dīn 'Aṭṭār
Foremost Deputy of Khwāja Bahā' al-Dīn Naqshband 70
Sayings of Khwāja 'Aṭṭār 72
Sayings of Khwāja Naqshband Transmitted by Khwāja 'Aṭṭār 76
Last Illness and Final Teachings of Khwāja 'Alā' al-Dīn 'Aṭṭār 77

Chief Companions and Deputies of Khwāja 'Alā' al-Dīn 'Aṭṭār 79
Khwāja Ḥasan 'Aṭṭār 79
Mawlānā Ḥusām al-Dīn Parsā al-Balkhī 81
Mawlānā Abū Sa'īd 82
Khwāja 'Ubaidallāh Imām al-Iṣfahānī 82
Shaikh 'Umar al-Bāyazīdī 83
Khwāja Aḥmad al-Samarqandī 83
Sayyid Sharīf al-Jurjānī 86
Mawlānā Niẓam al-Dīn Khāmūsh 87
Mawlānā Sa'd al-Dīn Kāshgharī 88

The Exceptional Khwāja 'Ubaidallāh al-Aḥrār (Tashkandī) 92
Khwāja Aḥrār's Family and Ancestors 92
His Childhood and Youth 94
His Spiritual Journey and the People He Met 98
Experiences with Sayyid Qāsim Tabrīzī 100
Meeting His Spiritual Director, Mawlānā Ya'qūb Charkhī 103
Some Sayings of Khwāja Aḥrār 104
Some Marvelous Exploits of Khwāja Aḥrār 108
His Death 110
Khwāja Aḥrār's Descendants and Companions 111
Khwāja Muḥammad ibn 'Abdallāh 111
Khwāja 'Abd al-Ḥaqq 111
Khwāja Muḥammad Yaḥyā 113
Mawlānā Sayyid Ḥasan 113
Mawlānā Sirāj al-Dīn Qāsim 114
Mīr 'Abd al-Awwal 114
Mawlānā Ja'far 115
Mawlānā Burhān al-Dīn Khuttalānī 115
Mawlānā Luṭfallāh Khuttalānī 116
Mawlānā Shaikh Idāmallāh 117
Mawlānā Sulṭān Aḥmad 117
Mawlānā Abū Sa'īd Awbahī 117

Mawlānā Muḥammad Qāḍī 118
Mawlānā Khwāja 'Alī Tashkandī 119
Shaikh Ḥabīb Najjār Tashkandī 120
Mawlānā Nūr al-Dīn Tashkandī 120
Mawlānā Zāda Otrārī 120
Mawlānā Nāṣir al-Dīn Otrārī 120
Hindū Khwāja Turkistānī 121
Mawlānā Ismā'īl Firhatī 121
The Spread of Khwāja Aḥrār's Influence to Anatolia 122
Shaikh Faḍlī Ilāhī 122
Sayyid Aḥmad al-Bukhārī 123
The Renowned Mawlānā 'Abd al-Raḥmān Jāmī 125
Mawlānā Jāmī's Education 127
His Sufi Initiation 128
The Sufis He Met 129
Mawlānā Jāmī's Meetings with Khwāja Aḥrār 129
His Pilgrimage to Mecca 131
Some Sayings 133
The Works of Mawlānā Jāmī 135
Selections from His Works 137
Poetry 137
From the Lawā'iḥ 140
From the Lawāmi' 140
His Death 141
Mawlānā Jāmī's Sons and Companions 142
Mawlānā 'Alī ibn Ḥusain Ṣafī 143
Appendix I: The Way of Liberation (*Iṭlāq*) in Islamic Sufism 145
Stages of the Way 146
Four Basic Practices of the Mystical Path 148
Remembrance 148
Austerity 149
Contrition 149
Fellowship 150
Commentary 150
Appendix II: Glossary of Sufi Terms 152
Bibliography 179

Foreword

The most common benefit of popular books is self-gratification. We either learn something or are entertained. That's what we love about them.

This book is not like that. In particular, the introduction, appendix, and glossary present unique concepts, and the perspicacious reader will pay special attention to them. The biographies themselves are taken directly from the *Rashaḥāt-i 'Ain al-Ḥayāt* and the *Nafaḥāt al-Uns min Ḥaḍarāt al-Quds*. Some Sufis from the Naqshband Order of Sufism may represent some of the characteristics of the Masters of Wisdom (Hâcegân Hânedâni). Please note that Naqshband lived in the fourteenth century and the period of the Masters of Wisdom started in the twelfth century. As for our modern times, for the past two hundred years, most Sufism is merely political, social.

This book teaches techniques on how to become an enemy to one's "self." The self is what generates our human perception. It's the stain on our soul that turns everything into a prey–predator game.

This book is all about perception . . . the perception that has no beginning, no end. We are the children of our perception. A separate physical universe doesn't exist; it has never been created. We represent merely a glimpse of the endless journey.

Being and becoming are the worst addiction for mankind. They lead to nothing but dead-end streets. This book shows the way out of that maze. We were born into the world where all opposites exist and multiply in different perceptions of good and bad, life and death, you and me. This book shows a way to make these opposites come together.

Instead of providing mental pleasure, this book points the way to Love and Ecstasy, through changing perception.

The knowledge in this book is not packaged and ready to go. It shows the way to trouble. It invites the reader to a long, hard journey. The cobblestones on its road have been paved by fire. Is it any wonder that there are only a few travelers around? But that is the only way: One has to be one's own martyr.

We are all going to die. One might as well die before his death. It's the only way to become immortal.

This book is all about it.

NEVIT ERGIN
SAN MATEO, CALIFORNIA
APRIL 2014

NEVIT O. ERGIN is the original English translator of the complete *Divan-i Kebir,* the author of *The Sufi Path of Annihilation* and *Tales of a Modern Sufi,* and the coauthor, with Will Johnson, of *The Forbidden Rumi* and *The Rubais of Rumi.* A Turkish-born surgeon, he has been an initiate in the Itlaq ("total liberation") path of Sufism under the tutelage of Sufi master Hasan Lutfi Shushud since 1955.

About the Author

An Autobiographical Note

My family have lived in Macedonia since the period of the conquests of Ottoman Sultan Murad II. My ancestors came from Konya in Central Asia Minor, where the mosque built by the Master Shaikh Hazret Abūlmaali Sadreddin Konevi contains his mausoleum and a cemetery for some Sufis, among whom is Shaikh Abdullah Bosnevi, interpreter of Ibn al-Arabi's *Fusus al-Hikam*.

My father, Avni Bey, was Defterdar of Izmir in Istanbul and was the first general manager of the Agricultural Bank at the institution of our Republic.

My spiritual life, beginning in 1917, is now 65 years old. I am satisfied with what, alone, the Almighty and His last Messenger deigned to honor this mortal servant. I do not deny the two or three guides I have had in different places. I am thankful to them; they are now dead. I learned French, English, and German. I am in the period when I pray to have an easy and faithful *muslim* death. (Who reaches the *root* in any Path receives the total impartiality in religions.)

HASAN LUTFI SHUSHUD
ISTANBUL 1982

HASAN LUTFI SHUSHUD was born in 1902 near Izmir in Anatolia, Turkey. A renowned Sufi saint and master, he was perhaps best known for his role as final guide to Gurdjieff's disciple J. G. Bennett. He died in 1988.

♦ About the Translator

Muhtar Holland (1935–2010), renowned translator of classical Arabic Islamic texts, was born in Durham, England. He embraced Islam in 1969 and adopted the name Muhtar, derived from the Arabic *Mukhtar* meaning "chosen." During his prolific career as a writer and translator he held several academic positions, including lecturing in Arabic, Turkish, and Near Eastern history at the University of Toronto; teaching Islamic law at the School of Oriental and African Studies, University of London; and classical Arabic and Greek philosophy at the Institute of Malay Language, Literature, and Culture of the National University of Malaysia. He was also a senior research fellow at the Islamic Foundation in Leicester, England.

Introduction

In the Name of God, All-Merciful and Compassionate

The aim of this book is to acquaint the reader with a community of saints and sages from the golden age of Islamic Sufism among the Turks. A serious effort has been made to present the subject in a realistic light, clear of the grotesque fantasies that have been woven around it in the past.

Islamic Sufism is divided into two main branches: the Northern Sufis and the Southern Sufis. The Northern group comprises the Aryan and Turanian sages who lived in East and West Turkestan, Transoxiana, Khurāsān, Iran, and Azerbaijan. The Khwājagān—Masters of Wisdom—were the basic component of this branch, although many other great mystics emerged in those regions, including Abū Yazīd (Bāyazīd) al-Bisṭāmī, Ḥamdūn al-Qaṣṣār, Junaid al-Baghdādī (who was originally from Nihāwand), Abū 'Alī al-Daqqāq of Nīshāpūr, Abū-l Ḥasan of Kharaqān, Abū-l Qāsim of Jurjān (Gurgān), Khwāja 'Abdallāh al Anṣārī of Herāt, Najm al-Dīn al-Kubrā, 'Alā' al-Dīn of Ardabīl, Shams al-Dīn of Tabrīz, Jalāl al-Dīn Rūmī, Sayyid Qāsim of Tabrīz, and many others.

The other branch is formed by the Sufis of Iraq, Syria, Arabia, and Africa. The Northern Sufis are distinguished from these (and from the Ottoman Sufis, who occupy an intermediate position) by their characteristic emphasis on the ecstatic realization of such primary concepts as liberation and occultation, annihilation of the self, permanent non-being, and non-existence. This emphasis is apparent in their temperamental disposition, their methods of training, their sayings, and their literature; it has enabled them to maintain their position at the forefront of all mystical endeavor, not only in Islam but throughout the world. The Southern Sufis present a sharp contrast, for they concern themselves with secondary notions like existential monism, union, love, manifestations and visions, unification, and so on.

The spiritual dynasty of the Masters of Wisdom lasted for five centuries. Its political contemporaries were the Khwārazm-Shāhs, Jenghis Khan, and Tamerlane and his successors. In the guise of the Naqshbandī Order it has continued in existence down to the present day.

The title of Khwāja or Master was first given in Central Asia, where it was conferred upon great scholars and sages, as well as on men of noble descent and worldly distinction. The first important figure to be recognized by this title was the venerable Yūsuf al-Hamadānī.

What did the Masters of Wisdom discover, and what did they impart?

They found that which is discovered by all who escape from illusion into Reality. They never withheld their discoveries from seekers who showed signs of promise. They lifted the veil of materialism and solved the riddle of creation. They achieved absolute deliverance. The significance of all this can be appreciated by those endowed with perspicacity.

Even today, they are ready to bring their truth to the aid of all who are capable of receiving it. Divine Abundance neither increases nor diminishes with time. The Age of Bliss is ever present and enduring. The Masters of Bliss do not stand aloof from the communities of mankind. The ways of realization, in all their purity, are still open to us now, provided we are ready to pass from imitation to verification. For Sufism consists in leaving metaphor for reality, in forsaking mere words in favor of direct experience. Such attainments call for talents of a high order, such as those that emerged over centuries among the Masters of Wisdom and their fellows of like disposition. Those rare individuals included Khwāja Naqshband, Muḥammad Parsā, Sa'd al-Dīn Kāshgharī, Mawlānā 'Abd al-Raḥmān Jāmī, and Khwāja 'Ubaidallāh al-Aḥrār. Their degree is that of absolute liberation, which is attained only by the renunciation of all relativities. In the words of Niyāzī-i Miṣrī, it is allotted "to one out of a thousand perfect men."

What doctrine or method is responsible for the mature development of the saints and sages we call the Masters of Wisdom?

It is the path of realization followed by those who cannot accept the Creation as a *fait accompli* and who reject the space-time world system. Such souls are the aspirants to genuine initiation. Their course is that of pure Sufism, which leads to God-consciousness and aims at transcending both existence and awareness.

This is the direct route of verification and realization. The goal of those who take this path is the shedding of all that is merely relative, escape from the cosmic illusion, attainment of absolute liberation, detachment from individualization. The starting point is annihilation in God (*fanā' fī-llāh*) and the destination is the Most Sacred Mystery of Non-Being (*ghaib*). This is pure Sufism, the prerogative of the most perfect beings, of the greatest Prophets. It is bestowed upon the Masters of Oneness, who have been divinely guided to weariness with being.

What is annihilation?

Annihilation (*fanā'*) is the essential basis of realization. Without it, contact with reality cannot be established; the veils that hide the true nature of things cannot be removed. Without annihilation, the cosmic illusion does not cease, the fictions of mind and memory are never ending.

Annihilation is to pass from phenomenal existence to real being, to the mystery of absolute liberation, to perceive the unreality and insubstantiality of the universe as it appears to exist; in short, to awaken.

It is generally supposed that annihilation means the merging of the creature in the Creator, of the servant in his Lord, so that both become unified. In reality, as Saint Abū ʻAlī al-Daqqāq declares, "it is bringing the being [*wujūd*] to ecstasy [*wajūd*]." (*Ecstasy* means "being on a transcendent plane.") In other words, it is the extinction of all that appears to exist, whether subjectively or objectively. It means passing from the concrete to the abstract.

Annihilation is achieved by very few, and it is reached by way of hardship and suffering. The degrees of annihilation are:

Annihilation of actions (*fanā' al-afʻāl*)
Annihilation of attributes (*fanā' al-ṣifāt*)
Annihilation of the Essence (*fanā' al-dhāt*)

To be transported from the realm of physical sensation to the spiritual realm is to achieve the annihilation of actions. The annihilation of attributes is the grade of relative occultation, the stage of potentiality and love. By attaining the annihilation of the Essence one is set free from existence and from the pitfalls of relative consciousness.

Intellectual problems concerning the nature of reality are resolved when one reaches the annihilation of actions, which is also called the "presence of knowledge." Emotional needs are satisfied in the annihilation of attributes, which is also known as the station of love. With the annihilation of the Essence, all occult problems disappear.

Annihilation reaches its consummation in permanent non-being, in the freedom of "as if it had never been." This transition can also be called the path of ecstasy or the way of Oneness. It is accessible exclusively to those who are subject to divine compulsion.

Annihilation is the fruit of rigorous self-discipline and contrition. Aptitude and perseverance are its prerequisites. When success is attained, the eternal ideas (*al-a'yān al-thābita*) are perceived. At the lowest level these are the objects of knowledge (*al-a'yān al-ʻilmiyya*), while on the highest plane they constitute occult substances (*al-a'yān al-ghaibiyya*). As the eternal ideas are the realities of the potentialities established in the Divine Consciousness, the visions experienced by aspirants who achieve annihilation are truly beatific.

On the way of realization, even loftier attainments lie ahead: transcendental vistas far surpassing any mental comprehension. To speak of these, we must have recourse to metaphors and a special terminology. Religious and esoteric truths are generally expressed on three levels of understanding. For those who have not achieved annihilation, symbolic examples are provided. For those who have made genuine progress on the mystical path, explanations are based on the experience of annihilation itself. For those who have attained permanent non-being, the state of non-existence supplies the key. For example, the concept of Divinity is perceived quite differently in each of these three grades. Similarly, such basic concepts as prophethood, sainthood, presences, materiality, spirituality, body, soul, and annihilation itself all transmute themselves into different realities on the various levels. Though essentially the same, they present themselves with different attributes.

In the rational and traditional sciences, progress is supposedly made by adding new knowledge to old. In esotericism, one advances from the coarse to the subtle, from existence to non-existence; that is, from potentiality to necessity. As Sufism is an ascent, through renunciation, from the corporeal to the Divine, a gradual penetration into the realm of absolute liberation brings one to the domain of miracles surpassing ordinary understanding. It has always been considered unwise to divulge the realities perceived there.

The Masters of Wisdom are among those who have accomplished this miraculous ascent. Steering well clear of mythical and superstitious nonsense, they represented Islamic Sufism in all its sublime purity.

The Reality of realities, the Truth of truths, in search of which mankind goes knocking in vain upon a thousand doors, has for centuries been discovered by men in the depths of their own God-given greatness. This they have achieved by way of annihilation and extinction, through non-being and non-existence, by forsaking the lines laid down by reason and tradition. Mysteries forever concealed from the "living" have surely been revealed to those who found the way to escape from the world of appearances into the realm of real discovery. They became free from all problems, whether mental, emotional, or occult. They came to know all there is to know, just as God Himself knows: with the Knowledge of Certainty, the Vision of Certainty, and the Truth of Certainty. This is the Essential Knowledge that comes with annihilation and permanent non-being (*fanā' wa-baqā*').

More important still: on this path a man becomes rapturously and ecstatically aware of the mysterious connection between the reality of man and the Nature of God. He understands the true significance of the concepts *creature* and *Creator.* He is privileged to drink of the waters of Paradise. From the state of a miserable underling, he returns to his primordial nobility and learns what it means to be raised to "the place on high."

I pray that Almighty God may help those who derive benefit from these pages to attain that priceless bliss. Amen. Amen. In honor of the Chief of God's Messengers.

From the shortcomings of my unworthy pen I take refuge in the spiritual grace of the great saints, and so I offer this humble work to the perspicacious and high-minded reader.

The Importance of Khwāja Yūsuf al-Hamadānī

Abū Ya'qūb Khwāja Yūsuf al-Hamadānī was born in 440/1048 at Būzanjird, near Hamadān. He died at Bāmiyīn in 535/1140, at the age of ninety-five (by the Islamic reckoning).* His tomb is in Merv.

He occupies a position of extraordinary importance in Turkish Sufism, since he represents the "top link" from which the "chains" of several major orders are suspended. In other words, he is the common starting-point for the lines of transmission of the Yasaviyya, the Naqshbandiyya, the Khwājagān, and—by way of Khwāja al-Yasavī and Luqmān Perendē—the Bektāshiyya.

> In his book entitled *Faṣl al-Khiṭāb,* the Cardinal Saint [*Quṭb*] Khwāja Muḥammad Parsā tells us that Mawlānā Sharaf al-Dīn al'Uqailī al-Anṣārī al-Bukhārī, a remarkable scholar and one of the great Masters of Wisdom, wrote in his noble hand: "Shaikh Yūsuf al-Hamadānī went to Baghdād at the age of eighteen. There he studied Islamic jurisprudence under the legist Abū Isḥaq, and achieved a first-class degree in philosophy. He followed the legal doctrines of the Supreme Imām, Abū Ḥanīfa, may Allāh be pleased with him. He

*Editor's note: When two dates are given, such as "440/1048," the first date refers to the Hijri calendar (also known as the Islamic or Muslim calendar), a lunar calendar beginning in the year 622 CE, the year of the emigration of the Prophet Muhammad from Mecca to Medina, known as the Hijra. The second date is that of the Gregorian or Western calendar.

furthered his studies at Iṣfahān and Bukhārā, and was well received in 'Irāq, Khurāsān, Khwārizm, and Transoxiana."*

His agnomen is Abū Ya'qūb. He was a religious leader, a scholar, and an adept in divine wisdom. He was endowed with an abundance of psychic experiences and talents, with charismatic powers and illustrious spiritual stations. First he went to Baghdād, where he attended the classes of Shaikh Abū Isḥāq al-Shīrāzī. Achieving high distinction, he surpassed his fellow students in jurisprudence and other subjects, especially philosophy.†

Young as Khwāja Yūsuf was, it seems that his teacher, Abū Isḥāq, considered him far above the average. He went on to study Prophetic Tradition under expert scholars in Baghdād, Samarqand, and Iṣfahān. At length, however, "he left all this and took to the path of worship, spiritual discipline and inner work."‡

Although he sat in the company of Shaikh 'Abdullāh al-Juwainī and Ḥasan al-Simnānī, the teacher who really trained him in Sufism was one of the most remarkable Sufis of Khurāsān—Shaikh Abū 'Alī al-Fārmadhī, the deputy of Abū-l Qāsim al-Gurgāni and spiritual director of Imām al-Ghazālī.

This is the chain of transmission linking Khwāja Yūsuf to the Prophet, on him be peace: Khwāja Yūsuf al-Hamadānī—Shaikh Abū 'Ali al-Fārmadhī—Abū-l Ḥasan Kharaqānī—Abū Yazīd al-Bisṭāmī—Imām Ja'far al-Ṣādiq—Imām Muḥammad al-Baqir—Imām Zain

---

*Quoted from *Rashaḥāt*. Editor's note: *Rashaḥāt-i 'Ain al-Ḥayāt* (Trickles from the Source of Life) is one of the primary sources regarding the Masters of Wisdom, originally written in Persian by Mawlānā 'Alī ibn Ḥusain Ṣafī (further details can be found in the bibliography).

†Quoted from *Nafaḥāt al-Uns*. Editor's note: another of the primary sources regarding the Masters of Wisdom, *Nafaḥāt al-Uns min Ḥaḍarāt al-Quds* (Breaths of Divine Intimacy) was originally written in Persian by Mawlānā 'Abd al-Raḥman Jāmī.

‡Editor's note: Throughout the book, unattributed quotations are given. These can be regarded as quotations from one of the source works listed in the bibliography, primarily *Rashaḥāt-i 'Ain al-Ḥayāt* or *Nafaḥāt al-Uns min Ḥaḍarāt al-Quds*.

al-'Ābidīn—Imām Ḥusain, the Martyr of Karbalā'—Imām 'Alī ibn Abī Ṭalib—the venerable Messenger, on him be peace.

Since Shaikh Abū 'Alī al-Fārmadhī came under the spiritual influence of Abū-l Qāsim al-Gurgānī of Ṭus, as well as that of the venerable Kharaqānī, Yūsuf al-Hamadānī has this second pedigree also: Khwāja Yūsuf al-Hamadānī—Shaikh Abū 'All al-Farmadhi-Abū-l Qāsim al-Gurgāni—Abū 'Uthmān al-Maghribī—'Alī Rūdbārī—Sarī al-Saqaṭī—Ma'rūf al-Karkhī—Imām al-Riḍā—Imām Mūsā al Kāẓim—Imām Ja'far al-Ṣādiq—Imām Muḥammad al-Bāqir—Imām Zain al-'Ābidīn—Imām Ḥusain—Imām 'Alī ibn Abī Ṭālib—the venerable Messenger, on him be peace.

According to *Risâle-i Bahâ'iyye,** "This line can also be traced back through Imām al-Qāsim, maternal grandfather of Imām Ja'far al-Ṣādiq, and thence by way of Salmān al-Fārisī and Abū Bakr al-Ṣiddīq to the venerable Messenger, on him be peace."

According to what Shaikh Awḥad al-Dīn al-Kirmānī told the venerable Muḥyi-l Dīn ibn al-'Arabī in 602/1205, Khwāja al-Hamadānī continued to give spiritual guidance for more than sixty years. Throughout this period he was an active teacher in 'Irāq, Khurāsān, and Transoxiana, spending a long time in Bukhārā. It was in this latter city, and in Samarqand, that his deputies, Khwāja Aḥmad al-Yasavī, 'Abd al-Khāliq al-Ghujdawānī, 'Abdullāh Barqī, and Ḥasan al-Andāqī, took their training from him. He divided the last part of his life between Herāt and Merv. In the month of Rabī'u-l'awwal, 535/1140, in the course of his final journey from Herāt to Merv, he passed away in the small town of Bāmiyīn. There he lay buried until one of his pupils, Ibn al-Najjār, had his remains transferred to Merv. His tomb in Merv is said to be a place of voluntary Pilgrimage.

By his own account, he was the author of two treatises, entitled "Stations of the Travelers" *(Manāzil al-Sā'irin)* and "Stations of the Wayfarers" *(Manāzil al-Sālikīn).* The story goes that in the year

*Editor's note: the *Risâle-i Bahâ'iyye* is a Turkish work by Rıf'at Bey, well described in the bibliography.

515/1121, as he was preaching to a large and important congregation at the Niẓāmiyya College in Baghdād, a famous jurist called Ibn al-Saqqā' got up and asked a question. The venerable Khwāja Yūsuf said: "Sit down, for you reek of unbelief. Maybe you will die outside the religion of Islam." This prediction was eventually proved correct. Ibn al-Saqqā' escorted a Byzantine ambassador back from Baghdād to Constantinople and there he died a Christian, having changed his religion in order to marry a princess.

Additional information about the venerable Khwāja Yūsuf al-Hamadani can be found in a biography of him attributed to his third deputy, Khwāja 'Abd al-Khāliq al-Ghujdawānī (entitled *Maqāmāt-i Yūsuf-i Hamadānī*). It seems he was a tall man, slightly built, with a swarthy and pockmarked complexion. He always wore patched woolen clothes. Attaching no importance to worldly affairs, he never consorted with the rich and powerful. He would accept nothing from anyone, but gave whatever came his way to those in need. He apparently did not know Turkish. He was cheerful, considerate, gentle, and compassionate. Whether sitting or on the move, he would be reciting the Qur'ān. Sometimes he would turn his face toward Hamadān, shedding many a tear. In divine remembrance (*dhikr/zikr*), he used the technique of retaining the breath, which he carried to such lengths that he would sweat profusely.

He was keeper of the staff and turban of Salmān al-Fārisī. The basic tenets of Islam he accepted without forced interpretation. He loved everybody, regardless of religion or creed. He used to visit the homes of Zoroastrians and members of other religions, explaining the true meaning and greatness of Islam.

He valued the poor above the rich. His own life was one of poverty. He took nothing for himself from the votive offerings and donations that came to his convent.* Great statesmen held him in high esteem. Sultan Sanjar looked up to him and paid him respect. In Ramaḍān of

*Editor's note: In the Sufi trandition, a *convent* is the abode of a master and his students.

the year 504/1111 this monarch sent Qāsim Jawqī from Samarqand with fifty thousand gold pieces for his center and his dervishes.

We know from the *Memorial* of Dawlat-Shāh that his convent in Merv was so renowned as to be called "the Ka'ba of Khurāsān." When Ḥakīm Sanā'ī came to Khurāsān from Ghazna, he affiliated himself to Yūsuf al-Hamadānī and spent some time at his center.

As he was breathing his last, Khwāja Yūsuf told Khwāja al-Yasavī to recite from the Qur'ān the Sūras *Yā-Sīn* and *al-Nāzi'āt*. He surrendered his spirit while the final Verses were being recited.

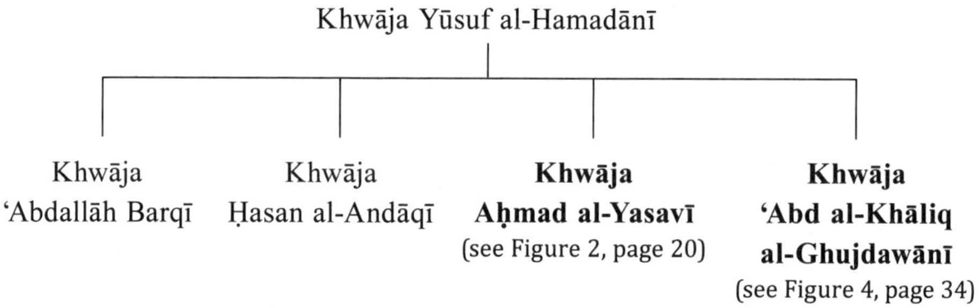

Figure 1

Note: In all the charts, **bold** indicates Masters who are heads of lineages that are depicted in later figures and are discussed in more detail later in the text. Not all shaikhs mentioned in the text will necessarily appear in these lineage charts. Those included in the charts illustrate the connections between the Masters given prominence in the text.

Three of the Deputies of Khwāja Yūsuf al-Hamadānī

♦ Khwāja 'Abdallāh Barqī

The first deputy of Khwāja Yūsuf al-Hamadānī was Khwāja 'Abdallāh Barqī. According to the *Rashaḥāt,* "He was originally from Khwārizm. He was learned and wise and endowed with charismatic gifts . . . His blessed tomb is situated in Bukhārā, next to the shrine of the venerable Shaikh Abū Bakr Isḥāq Gulābādī."

The date of his death is 555/1160.

♦ Khwāja Ḥasan al-Andāqī

The second deputy of Khwāja Yūsuf al-Hamadānī was Khwāja Ḥasan al-Andāqī. His agnomen is Abū Muḥammad, while his names are Ḥasan ibn Ḥusain al-Andāqī. Andāq is a village near Bukhārā. Born in the year 462/1069, he lived to the age of ninety, passing away on 26 Ramaḍān 552. His grandfather was 'Abd al-Karīm al-Andāqī, who had as his distinguished pupil the "Sun of the Imāms," Ḥulwānī.

According to the *Maqāmāt-i Yūsuf-i Hamadānī,* Ḥasan al-Andāqī was one of the eleven who accompanied Khwāja Yūsuf from Hamadān to Samarqand. According to the *Rashaḥāt*:

> He was the principal shaikh of his own day and age. He had agreeable techniques for inviting people to Divine Truth and for instructing his

disciples. He had an easy-going style, following the exemplary practice of the venerable Messenger in matters of worship and spiritual exercises. Having joined the company of Khwāja Yūsuf al-Hamadānī, he spent many years in his service. As one of the special intimates of Khwāja Yūsuf, he traveled with him as far as Khwārizm and Baghdād.

Also in the *Rashaḥāt,* the following account is attributed to Shaikh Sam'ānī, a follower of Khwāja Yūsuf al-Hamadānī:

> I first met him in Merv, at the convent of Khwāja Hamadānī, though I did not get to know him at that time. When I encountered him again later, in Bukhārā, I became his devoted servant and derived great benefit from his noble company. . . . He treated me with the utmost kindness. It was my blessing and good fortune to learn from him a number of Traditions handed down by our teacher and shaikh, Khwāja Yūsuf al-Hamadānī.

It is related that when the venerable Khwāja Ḥasan al-Andāqī became a follower and disciple in the service of the venerable Khwāja Yūsuf, his total dedication and diligent application to his tasks soon induced in him such a state of exaltation that he hardly paid any attention to the necessities of everyday life, neglecting his livelihood and the welfare of his family. One day the venerable Khwāja Yūsuf offered him this advice:

> "You are a poor man, with dependants to support. You have a personal obligation to attend to your basic needs, the neglect of which is neither reasonable nor in accordance with sacred law." In response to this, Khwāja Ḥasan said: "In my present state, I am somehow powerless to deal with anything else."
>
> These words annoyed Khwāja Yūsuf, who rebuked Khwāja Ḥasan. That night, however, he saw a vision in which God, Glorified and Exalted is He, addressed him, saying: "Yūsuf, We have given you the

> eye of the mind, but We have given Ḥasan both the eye of the mind and the eye of the heart."*

After this dream, Khwāja Yūsuf al-Hamadānī is said to have held Khwāja Ḥasan in the highest regard and esteem, never again offering any suggestion concerning his worldly affairs.

Khwāja Ḥasan's tomb lies to the east of Shaikh Gulābādī's shrine, on Marsh Hill in Bukhārā.

♦ Khwāja Aḥmad al-Yasavī, "Top Link" for the Turkish Shaikhs

Khwāja Aḥmad al-Yasavī is one of the celebrated Turkish shaikhs living in Central Asia in the fifth and sixth centuries of the Islamic era. He was born in Sayram,† a small town on the Karasu in the Tarim Basin, in the Chinese Province of East Turkestan, around the middle of the fifth century. According to traditional accounts, he reached the age of 120 before passing away in Yasi in the year 562/1166.

> He was the third deputy of Khwāja Yūsuf al-Hamadānī. His birthplace, Yasi, is a famous city in Turkestan. All his connections are with this area, and the blessed tomb of the venerable Khwāja is situated there too. The people of Turkestan call him Khwāja Ata Yasavī. *Ata* means "father" in the Nüvâi dialect, but they apply it to the great Turkish shaikhs.
>
> The venerable Khwāja Aḥmad was endowed with splendid charismatic powers and lofty spiritual degrees. At a very tender age he familiarized himself with the remarkable alchemical works of the venerable Baba Arslan. It is related that Baba Arslan occupied himself with the Khwāja's education after receiving a sign from the Bringer of Good Tidings, the venerable Messenger, on him be peace,

**Rashaḥāt.*

†According to the *Rashaḥāt,* in Yasi (which is now called Tashkent).

> and that the Khwāja made excellent progress while serving him as a novice. As long as Baba Arslan was alive, Khwāja Aḥmad remained his devoted servant. After his tutor's death, he followed his instructions and went to Bukhārā, where he completed his training in the service of Khwāja Yūsuf al-Hamadānī, qualifying with full honors as a teacher in his own right.*

His father was Shaikh Ibrāhīm, one of the prominent shaikhs of Sayram, while his mother, Lady 'Ā'isha, was the daughter of Shaikh Mūsā, one of Shaikh Ibrāhīm's deputies. Khwāja Aḥmad was seven years old when his father died. His mother having died even earlier, he was brought up by his only sibling, his elder sister Lady Gawhar Shahnāz. Shaikh Ibrāhīm's pedigree goes back to the venerable Imām 'Alī ibn Abī Ṭālib, by way of Khwāja Isḥāq Baba, Shaikh of shaikhs, Ocean of Wisdom, Peak of Tranquillity, Cardinal Saint of Turkestan.

> In a treatise by a certain shaikh of modern times, it is stated that after the passing of Khwāja 'Ubaidullāh Barqī and Khwāja Ḥasan al-Andāqī, the vicarship passed to Khwāja Aḥmad al-Yasavī, who engaged in missionary work in Bukhārā. After a while, he received an indication from the Unseen, requiring him to go to Turkestan. Before setting out for Yasi, he instructed all his associates to follow the lead of Khwāja 'Abd al-Khāliq al-Ghujdawānī. It is no secret that the venerable Khwāja Aḥmad al-Yasavī, sanctified be his soul, is the "top link" for all the Turkish shaikhs and that most of the eminent Sufis of Turkestan are affiliated to him. Many saints have arisen from his noble line.†

It would appear, therefore, that after the deaths of Khwāja Yūsuf al-Hamadānī (535/1140) and his first two successors, Khwāja Ḥasan al-Andāqī (552/1157) and Khwāja 'Abdullāh Barqī (555/1160), Aḥmad

---

**Rashaḥāt.*

†Rashaḥāt.

al-Yasavī remained for some time at his teaching post in Bukhārā, then returned to Yasi near the end of his life and spent his last days in his native land. He was widely renowned among his contemporaries in those regions. Many people came to him for guidance and, as a means of instructing them in morals, sacred law, mysticism, and spiritual reality, he would compose rhymed and metrical aphorisms in Eastern Turkish. These verses (three hundred and sixty in all, according to one of his aphorisms) were written in a popular style, appealing to the mentality of ordinary folk. Under the title *Divân-i Hikmet* they have been printed again and again in Chagatay Turkish, in Kazan, Tashkent, and Istanbul. This work has been standard reading for centuries among the Asiatic Turks.

All the verses in this work contain advice on how to attain to Reality by way of piety and devotion, discipline and inner work. They recount the hardships on the path of Love. They make detachment from worldly ties a precondition of spiritual progress. Apart from those aphorisms that expound the Qur'ān and the exemplary conduct of the Prophet, reconcile the principles of Sufism and sacred law, or explain to ecstatics the necessity of obedience, many of the verses collected in the *Divân* are pieces composed in praise of the venerable Messenger, on him be peace, or of the Supreme Imām and other great men, while some are about acts of faith, conditions in the Hereafter, and the manners and customs of the Sufi orders. We cannot know for certain whether or not the entire contents are attributable to Khwāja Yasavī. The tone of the work is one of restraint and earnestness. There is an absence of ecstatic utterances, whereas pleas for forgiveness, supplications, and entreaties are frequent.

The following is one of Khwāja Aḥmad's earliest poems (from Khāzinī's *Jawāhir al-Abrār*):

My Maker I'll seek in this universe by night and day;
From the four directions of space I have been torn
away.
Let me go from four to seven; one by one to nine I'll
count.

In Saturn's sphere, from two on up to ten I've made my way;
Three hundred and sixty the rivers I crossed, the mountains four hundred and forty-four.
*I drank the wine of Unity and fell inside the glass.**
But when I fell inside, I found the emptiness was full,
For there I saw a hundred thousand wise men circling round.
I walked among them, asked about the object of my quest;
To my amazement, they all said: "It lies within yourself!"
Such pain and anguish did I feel when, deep within the sea,
I saw the pearl a-bleeding lie, within its oyster shell.
Poor Khwāja Aḥmad's soul is the pearl and its blood alike.
His place is everywhere, within that Nowhere beyond place.

The saintly reputation of Khwāja Aḥmad al-Yasavī has endured for centuries in Turkestan, Transoxiana, Khwārizm, along the banks of the Volga (Itil), and in Anatolia, for he played a leading role in spreading Islamic Sufism among the Turks in Asia. His wise aphorisms were well suited, both in style and in content, to the tastes and level of understanding prevalent among the people of those countries, while he was known to be a Sufi of advanced personal attainment. For these reasons, he is considered to be the fountain-head of a wide range of Sufi orders, such as the Yasaviyya, the Khwājagān, the Naqshbandiyya, and the Bektāshiyya.

---

*Translator's note: there is a play on the word *meydan,* which means (*a*) (Persian *mey-dān*) "a vessel for wine," and (*b*) (Arabic *maydān*) "open space; arena; the environment; the universe; space where dervishes perform dhikr."

The additional information gleaned from the *Divân-i Hikmet* and from legendary accounts can reasonably be summarized as follows: through the mediation of Khiḍr, on him be peace, that is, through the Guidance existing from all eternity, the young Khwāja Yasavī came to the notice of Shaikh Baba Arslan, who was then still living in Sayram. Baba Arslan passed away soon after this, however, which meant that Khwāja Yasavī's early development as a Sufi was essentially acquired by heredity. At the age of twenty-seven he therefore attached himself to the famous Khwāja Yūsuf al-Hamadāni in Bukhārā.

In Bukhārā he also studied the exoteric sciences, becoming one of the experts of his day in rationalistic and traditional scholarship alike. It seems he "would not take a crumb" from the votary offerings and donations that reached his convent, preferring to make his own living by carving spoons. We are told that the Khwāja's ox used to hawk his spoons and ladles around the town, carrying them in a saddlebag on its back. If any buyer failed to put some payment, in money or in kind, into the saddlebag, the ox would follow the customer around until he paid up. As recorded in the *Rashaḥāt*, "That ox would go around each day until the evening prayer, then the venerable Khwāja would come and collect the takings with his own blessed hand."

On reaching the age of sixty-three, he had a cell constructed at his convent in Yasi, six feet below ground. There he spent the rest of his days in teaching and worship, out of respect for the lifespan of the noble Messenger.

The legends record the wonders he performed for friends and opponents. The venerable Amīr Timūr Gurgān was a firm believer in him. It was he who had the Khwāja's mausoleum built in Yasi, acting on instructions received in a dream. According to the *Wāqi'āt-ı Timūr,* Amīr Timūr consulted the Khwāja's *Maqāmāt* as an oracle before going into action against Beyazid, "the Thunderbolt," at the battle of Ankara. He came across this good omen:

Whenever you encounter difficulties, recite the following quatrain:

A candle on the longest night lights up the room;
At once the world becomes a rose garden in bloom.
This task of mine is hard enough—ease my way soon!
There's not one thing so hard it cannot ease assume.

Says Amīr Timūr: "I committed this quatrain to memory. When I was in combat with the army of the Byzantine Emperor, I recited it seventy times and came out victorious."*

**Rashaḥāt* and F. Köprülü, *Türk Edebiyyâtında Ilk Mütesavvifler.*

The Chain of Transmission of the Yasaviyya

Through the Four Deputies of Khwāja Aḥmad al-Yasavī

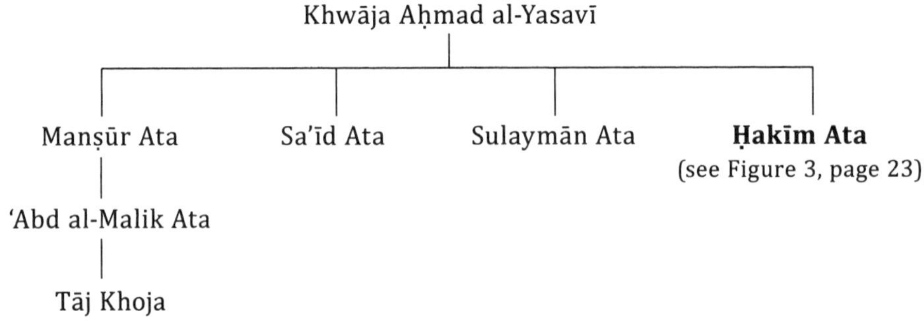

Figure 2

The line goes back from Khwāja Yūsuf al-Hamadānī: to Khwāja Abū 'Alī al-Fārmadhī and from him to Shaikh Abū-l Qāsim al-Gurgānī. Two chains connect the latter with the venerable 'Alī ibn Abī Ṭālib:

1. via Shaikh Abū-l Ḥasan Kharaqānī, Abū Yazīd al-Bisṭāmī, and Imām Ja'far al-Ṣādiq;
2. via Shaikh 'Uthmān al-Maghribī, Abū 'Alī al-Kātib, Abū 'Alī Rūdbārī, Junaid al-Baghdādī, and Sarī al-Saqaṭī.

Lines of descent: one line of succession comes down through Ḥakīm Ata and Zengi Ata, then splits into two branches under Sayyid Ata and Ṣadr Ata. A third branch leads by way of Qāsim Shaikh and Khalīl Ata to the venerable Khwāja Bahā' al-Dīn Naqshband, while a fourth line brings us from Luqmān Perendē down to Saint Ḥajjī Bektāsh.

♦ Manṣūr Ata and His Family Lineage

Manṣūr Ata was the first deputy of Khwāja Yasavī. The son of Baba Arslan, he was versed in exoteric and esoteric science. He began his education under Baba Arslan. When his father died, he followed his advice and entered the service of Khwāja Aḥmad, in which he achieved sainthood. He left this world in the year 594/1197.

'Abd al-Malik Ata was the son of Manṣūr Ata and grandson of Baba Arslan. Having succeeded his father, he devoted himself to "the training of students and the guidance of travelers on the Path of Truth." He is also known as 'Abd al-Malik Khoja. His son, Tāj Khoja, was the father of Zengi Khoja.

Tāj Khoja studied the Sufi Path and Reality, receiving instruction also from his father. "Having achieved a first-class degree, he became qualified to give guidance to seekers."

♦ Sa'īd Ata of Khwārizm

Sa'īd Ata was the second deputy of Khwāja Yasavī, on whose instructions he worked as a teacher. A native of Khwārizm, he died in 615/1218.

♦ Sulaymān Ata, Great Turkish Shaikh

Sulaymān Ata, third deputy of Khwāja Aḥmad al-Yasavī, was one of the great Turkish shaikhs. He lived at Ak-Kurgan in the province of Khwārizm, where he spent a long period in the role of spiritual guide, inviting the people to Divine Truth. According to the traditional account, he predeceased the other deputies of the venerable Yasavī, dying in the year 582/1282.*

He was buried in Ak-Kurgan (also known as Bakirgan), and we are told, "His blessed tomb is still famous. People in need derive benefit from making pious visitation there." His Sufi sayings, in Turkish, are widely known in Turkestan. These include the advice: "Treat everyone you meet as Khiḍr and every night as the Night of Power." Equally famous is the reply he gave concerning self-mortification, in response to subtle esoteric queries addressed to the shaikhs of Turkestan by the Sufis of Iraq:

All is ripe; 'tis we who are raw.
All is wheat; 'tis we who are straw.

♦ Ḥakīm Ata

Ḥakīm Ata was the fourth deputy of Khwāja Yasavī. He is well known among the Turks of Central Asia and the Volga Basin for his Sufi poetry and hymns, as well as for his pious writings, which discuss such topics as the Resurrection, the Antichrist, and the end of time.† According to the *Rashaḥāt*, "For many years after the first three successors, he occupied his teaching post and invited people to Divine Truth."

His exploits are described in detail in a popular work entitled *The Book of Ḥakīm Ata.* Many marvels and miracles are attributed to him, as well as to Ḥubbī Khoja, one of his three sons.

*Editor's note: On the previous page Shushud writes that the other deputies died in 1197 and 1218, thus predeceasing Sulaymān Ata. This text reflects the original.
†F. Köprülü

The Line of Transmission through Zengi Ata, Deputy of Ḥakīm Ata

Figure 3

Zengi Ata, also known as Zengi Baba, is the greatest and best known of Ḥakīm Ata's deputies. The son of Tāj Khoja, his black skin betokened his descent from Arslan Baba, the Arab.* He was born in the province of

*Translator's note: *Arab* in Turkish often means "Negro."

Shash (Tashkent), where he lived until his death in 656/1258. His tomb is there also. It seems that "needy people who visit it have their wishes fulfilled." According to the *Rashaḥāt,* "We have it from Mawlānā Qāḍī, on him be God's mercy, that the venerable Khwāja 'Ubaidullāh, sanctified be his soul, said: 'Whenever I visit the tomb of Zengi Ata, I hear the cry "Allāh, Allāh" issuing from the shrine.'"

For a long time he enjoyed the spiritual direction of his father, Tāj Khoja, but when the latter died he entered the service of Ḥakīm Ata, "in accordance with an indication from the Unseen." On the death of Ḥakīm Ata, he married his teacher's widow, Anber Ana, the daughter of Bughra (or Barak) Khān. We are told that this union produced "sons and grandsons, all of whom were both learned and active, each one of them being an example and guide for the travelers and seekers of his generation."

Zengi Ata is said to have concealed his true condition by making his living as an oxherd in the vicinity of Tashkent.

♦ The Deputies of Zengi Ata: Uzun Ḥasan Ata, Sayyid Ata, Ṣadr Ata, and Badr Ata

Uzun Ḥasan Ata, Sayyid Ata, Ṣadr Ata, and Badr Ata were students at one of the colleges of Bukhārā when "they happened to feel the urge, one night, to embark on a spiritual quest. In the morning, they gathered their belongings, left the college, and set out toward Turkestan, where they entered the service of Zengi Ata." In the desert near Tashkent "they saw a thicklipped Negro herdsman pasturing a herd of oxen. That person was none other than the venerable Zengi Ata."

Because of their perfect submissiveness, Ḥasan Ata and Ṣadr Ata progressed more rapidly in their training than the other two. Sayyid Ata and Badr Ata were held back by the pride they took in their noble ancestry and learning. Nevertheless, all four eventually won the affectionate favor of Zengi Ata and became qualified to teach.

Sayyid Aḥmad Ata is said to have been endowed with supernatural powers:

According to the biography of Khwāja Bahā'al-Dīn Naqshband, the venerable Khwāja relates that a farmer was once sowing millet when along came Sayyid Aḥmad Ata, who asked him what he was doing and what he was sowing. "I am sowing millet," the farmer replied, "but this field gives a poor harvest." The venerable Sayyid Ata thereupon addressed the ground, saying: "Land, yield good millet!" For many years thereafter, they tell us, that field produced a good crop of millet without a seed being sown.

♦ The Deputies of Sayyid Ata

Ismā'īl Ata

Ismā'īl Ata was one of the great deputies of Sayyid Aḥmad Ata. According to the venerable Khwāja 'Ubaidullāh Aḥrār,* "At first, people were critical of Ismā'īl Ata. But the Ata would say: 'I pay no attention to this. I give them food and play the drum for them. I am ready to sacrifice my life for those who truly understand my words.'"†

Ismā'īl Ata lived in the region of Khuzyān, which lies between Sayram and Tashkent. Explaining the meaning of kindness and compassion, he used to say: "Be a shade in the sun, a cloak in the cold, and bread in time of famine." According to Khwāja 'Ubaidullāh Aḥrār, the whole of the Ata's teaching is summed up in this saying.

Khwāja 'Ubaidullāh Aḥrār used to say: "Sayyid Sharīf al-Jurjānī would say to me: 'O son-of-a-shaikh, the aroma of true experience comes from the worship of Ismā'īl Ata's disciples.'"‡

Isḥāq Khoja

Isḥāq Khoja is said to have been "an exceptionally enlightened character." He lived in the small town of Isbijāb between Tashkent and Sayram. He was one of the great deputies of Sayyid Ata. Shaikh 'Abdullāh Khūjandī tells us how he came to him for instruction,

---

*Please see the chapter devoted to Khwāja 'Ubaidullāh Aḥrār and his writings later in the book.

†Recounted in the *Rashaḥāt.*

‡*Rashaḥāt.*

some time before becoming a disciple of Khwāja Bahā'al-Dīn Naqshband:

> I asked the whereabouts of Isḥāq Khoja and they told me he was in Isbijāb. I joined his company as a seeker, not mentioning anything about the events of Tirmidh.* For several days I remained in his service. He had a young son, whose features bore the mark of discernment and whose blessed brow showed the signs of felicity. One day, he interceded with his father on my behalf, saying: "This dervish is in need. It is fitting that he be honored by your nobly accepting him into your noble service." But Isḥāq Khoja replied: "My son, this dervish should become the disciple of Khwāja Naqshband. It is not for us to take him in hand . . ." On hearing these words, I returned to Khūjand. There I awaited the appearance of the venerable Khwāja, until such time as I had the honor of serving him in Bukhārā.†

♦ Kamāl Shaikh Īkānī

By way of Ayman Baba, Shaikh 'Alī, and Mawdūd Shaikh, the chain of transmission reaches Kamāl Shaikh Īkānī, who lived in the province of Tashkent. The Īkāniyya is the principal branch of the Yasaviyya.

> According to Khwāja Aḥrār, "Kamāl Shaikh was the pupil of Mawdūd Shaikh and a fellow dervish of Khādim Shaikh. Kamāl Shaikh often came to see us after we had returned from Khurāsān and settled in Tashkent. It was on one of these visits that the venerable Khwāja told us to demonstrate the 'sawing dhikr' for the benefit of the shaikh. (The "dhikr of the saw" is a form of divine remembrance commonly practiced among the Turkish shaikhs. It takes its name from the rasping sound produced in the throats of those who are working at it.)

---

*Some time before he found Khwāja Naqshband, Shaikh 'Abdullāh visited the tomb of Ḥakīm al-Tirmidhī, in Tirmidh. There he received this spiritual message: "Turn back. The object of your quest will appear in Bukhārā twelve years from now." This was a prediction of the emergence of Bahā'al-Dīn Naqshband.

†*Rashaḥāt* and *Nafaḥāt*.

> Kamāl Shaikh performed the dhikr seven or eight times in imitation of the dervishes, using all his energy. When the venerable Khwāja said: 'Enough!' we had begun to feel the strain on our hearts." By some accounts, the intensity of it was all-consuming.*

After Kamāl Shaikh, the *Tibyān* mentions Shaikh 'Alī Ābādī, Shams Özkendī, Abdāl Shaikh, Shaikh 'Abd al-Wāsi', and (living in Tashkent in 974) Shaikh 'Abd al-Muhaymin.

♦ Khadim Shaikh

One of the companions of Mawdūd Shaikh, he was engaged in spiritual teaching in Tashkent and Transoxiana at the time when Khwāja 'Ubaidallāh al-Aḥrār first appeared on the scene. He gave guidance to many disciples and met with Khwāja 'Ubaidallāh. These wise sayings of his, transmitted by his deputy and lieutenant Shaikh Jamāl al-Dīn al-Bukhārī, are recorded in the *Rashaḥāt*:

> It is possible for a dervish to achieve the state of composure we reach at the end of dhikr, even without passing through all its stages. However, this kind of composure is impermanent; lacking stability, it quickly dissolves into natural cheerfulness. The stages of the dhikr correspond to the subtle bodies. By passing through them all—and thereby experiencing certain illuminations and revelations—the dervish may attain a state entirely unaffected by ordinary impulses and distracting thoughts.
>
> In the state of *samā'* [audience (with the divine)], the Universal Intellect emanates from the divine realm to this partial intellect and becomes ruler of the kingdom that is the dervish's physical being. Since it lies within the power of the Universal Intellect to grasp and control the entire universe all at once, it is a relatively trivial matter to govern the body of a human being. Without doubt, the body of the dervish then becomes, as it were, the protectorate of the Universal Intellect, so that his ritual purity is rendered inviolate. The faithful

**Rashaḥāt.*

disciple then becomes immune, to a certain degree, to the laws of nature so that ordinary human needs cannot manifest in him. It is therefore quite unnecessary for his ritual purity to be renewed through ablution.

As soon as the faithful disciple has cleansed and polished all worldly allure from the mirror of his heart and has purified its innermost apartment of all but God, he immediately begins to experience a selfless rapture which obliterates his own being and that of the unreal world. This purification is the prelude to selflessness. Such loss is true finding. The Sufis call this self-forgetting "non-being" [*'adam*] or "absence" [*ghaiba*]. This state is the prelude to the dawn of bliss and union. After losing himself in this fashion and discovering a genuine form of being, a dervish is incapable of reverting to ordinary human existence.

Once one has acquired a divinely endowed mode of being, one is liberated from the troubles of personal and worldly existence.

This state is called "permanence after annihilation" [*baqā' ba'da-lfanā*].

According to the *Tibyān,* the line of transmission from Khādim Shaikh and then Shaikh Jamāl al-Dīn al-Bukhārī is as follows: Shaikh Kharīdār 'Azīzegī—Mawlānā Gūhzarīnī—Shaikh Qāsim Germīnī—Muḥammad Mu'min Samarqandī—Shaikh Ākhund—Mullā 'Azīzān.

Khwāja 'Abd al-Khāliq al-Ghujdawānī

Fourth Deputy of Khwāja Yūsuf al-Hamadānī

The name Khwāja 'Abd al-Khāliq al-Ghujdawānī heads the list in the biographies of the Masters of Wisdom, for he is the chief and top link of this chain of transmission. One of the great shaikhs of Turkestan, he was the fourth deputy of Khwāja Yūsuf al-Hamadānī and one of the eleven who accompanied Khwāja Yūsuf from Hamadān to Samarqand. He is said to have bestowed his spiritual influence on the venerable Khwāja Bahā' al-Dīn Naqshband.

He was born in Ghujdawān, and his tomb is in the same place:

> Ghujdawān is a town or large village six or seven miles from Bukhārā. His father's name was 'Abd al-Jamīl. Known in his own time as 'Abd al-Jamīl Imām, he was a descendant of Imām Mālik. He had many followers and possessed a remarkable ability for solving problems. He was versed in exoteric and esoteric knowledge alike and pursued the path of right guidance in conformity with Qur'ān and Sunna. He was from the town of Malatya in Anatolia. His mother was a Seljuq princess. 'Abd al-Jamīl Imām is reputed to have been on intimate terms with Khiḍr, on him be peace, who congratulated him on the Khwāja's spiritual stature and told him to give him the name 'Abd al-Khāliq.*

**Rashaḥāt.*

In the course of events 'Abd al-Khāliq's father moved from Anatolia to Transoxiana, settling in Ghujdawān near Bukhārā, where the boy was born and grew up. He was studying in Bukhārā when, by his own account, "I was twenty years of age when the Master of the righteous, the venerable Khiḍr, on him be peace, commended me to the great Shaikh Khwāja Yūsuf al-Hamadānī and advised him to give me instruction. I served as his novice as long as he was in Transoxiana, to my practical and spiritual benefit."

When Khwāja Yūsuf al-Hamadānī went back to Khurāsān, Khwāja 'Abd al-Khāliq engaged in ascetic practices, which he followed in a private manner. His saintliness and charismatic powers were outstanding. According to the *Rashaḥāt*, "He gained many disciples in the province of Damascus and a dervish convent and center were established in his name."

♦ Khwāja 'Abd al-Khāliq's Letter of Counsel

The following instructions appear in a Letter of Counsel, which he wrote for his third deputy Khwāja Awlīyā' Kabīr:

> You should thoroughly imbue yourself with knowledge, self-discipline and piety. Make a profound study of the Islamic classics. Learn jurisprudence and the Prophetic Traditions. Steer clear of ignorant zealots. Always perform your ritual prayer in congregation, but do not act as prayer-leader or muezzin.
>
> Do not seek fame, for in fame lies calamity.
>
> Do not get involved in other people's affairs. Do not frequent the company of kings and princes.
>
> Do not build a dervish convent or live in one. Do not engage too often in sacred music and dance, for over-indulgence in this is fatal to the life of the heart. But do not reject the sacred dance, for many are attached to it.
>
> Speak little, eat little, and sleep little. Avoid the crowd and pre-

serve your solitude. Do not converse with young people, women, the rich, or the worldly. Eat lawful food and avoid suspect provisions. Postpone marriage as long as you can, for its worldly demands will be detrimental to your religious life.

Do not laugh excessively, for undue hilarity deadens the heart.

Treat everyone kindly and look down on no one. Do not embellish your outward appearance, for ornament is a mark of inner poverty. Do not get into quarrels. Ask favors of none and do not let yourself become a burden to others.

Place no trust in this world and do not rely on worldly people. Let your heart be filled with melancholy and disillusion; let your body suffer and your eyes weep. Let your conduct be upright and your prayers sincere. Wear old clothes and choose a poor man as your companion. Let your home be a house of worship and let the Exalted Truth be your most intimate friend.

♦ The Principles of the Way of the Masters

The following aphorisms, composed by Khwāja 'Abd al-Khāliq, are considered to be the principles of the Way of the Masters:

1. Conscious breathing (*hōsh dar dam*): Remain attentive with every breath. According to Sa'd al-Dīn Kāshgharī: "Be conscious and heedful of God, Glorified and Exalted is He, with every breath you take." In this context Shaikh Najm al-Dīn al-Kubrā said:

> The "h" in the divine name Allāh is the very sound we make with every breath. The other letters (in the Arabic spelling: *alif* and reduplicated *lām*) represent an intensified definite article (serving to emphasize the Uniqueness of God). The essential part of the divine name is therefore that "h," which automatically accompanies our every breath. All life depends on the constant utterance of that noble name.

The venerable Makhdūmī (Mawlānā Jāmī) was obviously alluding to Loss of Separate Identity (*ghaib al-huwīya*) in his stanza:

Your alphabet I'm sure you know
We lose ourselves in "h" with every breath we blow
Utter it carefully and be awake:
That is no ordinary sound you make!

In Sufi terminology "Loss of Separate Identity" is an expression for non-individualization [*lā ta'ayyun*], referring to the indefinable Essence of the Glorified and Exalted Truth. We are speaking of genuine transformation through liberation from all limitation; since this transcends the confines of all knowledge and perception, it represents the Absolute Unknowable.*

2. Watch your step! (*naẓar bar qadam*): Direct yourself constantly toward your goal.
3. Journey homeward (*safar dar waṭan*): Pass from the world of potentiality to the world of realization.
4. Solitude in the crowd (*khalwat dar anjuman*): Be free from limitation in the midst of limitations. When Khwāja Naqshband was asked to state the basic principle of spiritual development, he said: "Solitude in the crowd; that is being outwardly with people, but inwardly with God, Exalted is He." According to Khwāja Awlīyā' Kabīr, it means that one should reach the stage where one is so constantly and completely absorbed in divine remembrance that "one could walk through the market-place without hearing a sound."
5. Remembrance (*yād kard*): Remember with the heart at the same time as mentioning with the tongue—or transforming dhikr of the tongue into dhikr of the heart. According to Khwāja 'Ubaidallāh al-Aḥrār, "the real meaning of dhikr is inward awareness of God, Exalted is He. The purpose of dhikr is to attain this consciousness."
6. Returning (*bāz gasht*): Single-minded pursuit of divine Truth. According to Khwāja Aḥrār, it means the return to God.

**Rashaḥāt.*

7. Attentiveness (*nigāh dāsht*): Keeping out worldly thoughts by vigilant control of one's attention.
8. Recollection (*yād dāsht*): Constant awareness in the blissful presence of God, Exalted is He. "The complete experience of divine contemplation, achieved through the action of objective Love."

The *Rashaḥāt* also mentions three additional terms, namely:

9. Awareness of time (*wuqūf zamānī*): Watching one's composure and checking one's tendency to heedlessness. According to the venerable Ya'qūb Charkhī, Khwāja Naqshband explained this as "seeking forgiveness when in a state of spiritual constriction and expressing gratitude when in a state of expansion."
10. Awareness of number (*wuqūf 'adadī*): Observing the exact number of repetitions in dhikr. Khwāja 'Alā' al-Dīn al-'Aṭṭār said: "The important thing is not the number of repetitions but rather the composure and awareness with which one makes them." According to Khwāja Bahā' al-Dīn Naqshband, numerical awareness is the first stage of esoteric knowledge.

> The distinction between Knowledge of Certainty and lesser esoteric knowledge is this: Knowledge of Certainty means direct perception of the light of the Divine Essence and attributes, whereas lesser esoteric knowledge relates to verbal understanding and the apprehension of meaning through inspiration from God, Glorified and Exalted is He.*

11. Awareness of the heart (*wuqūf qalbī*): Equivalent to Recollection (as in 8, above). Khwāja Aḥrār says it means that the heart becomes aware of God, Glorified and Exalted is He. The heart is the comprehensive human entity within which all other organs and faculties are contained. "It is the divine manuscript on which infinite mysteries are recorded."

We read in *Nafaḥāt al-Uns* that Khwāja 'Abd al-Khāliq Ghujdawānī was regarded as an authority by all the Sufi orders and that he kept on

**Rashaḥāt.*

good terms with people of all classes. He was always careful to follow the prescriptions of Islamic law and to avoid heretical innovations. In his youth, he had learned the dhikr of the heart from none other than Khwāja Khiḍr, on him be peace, who had adopted him as a son. He later entered the service of Khwāja Imām Abū Ya'qūb Yūsuf al-Hamadānī, where he remained until the death of that wise and learned Shaikh of shaikhs. He used to say that there is no escape from the forces of sensuality and egoism until one reaches the final stage of annihilation.

Four deputies succeeded him: Khwāja Aḥmad Ṣiddīq, Khwāja Awlīyā' Kabīr, Khwāja Sulaymān Germīnī, and Khwāja 'Ārif Riwgarī. The *Thamarāt al-Fu'ād* mentions a fifth deputy, Khwāja Khubbāz.

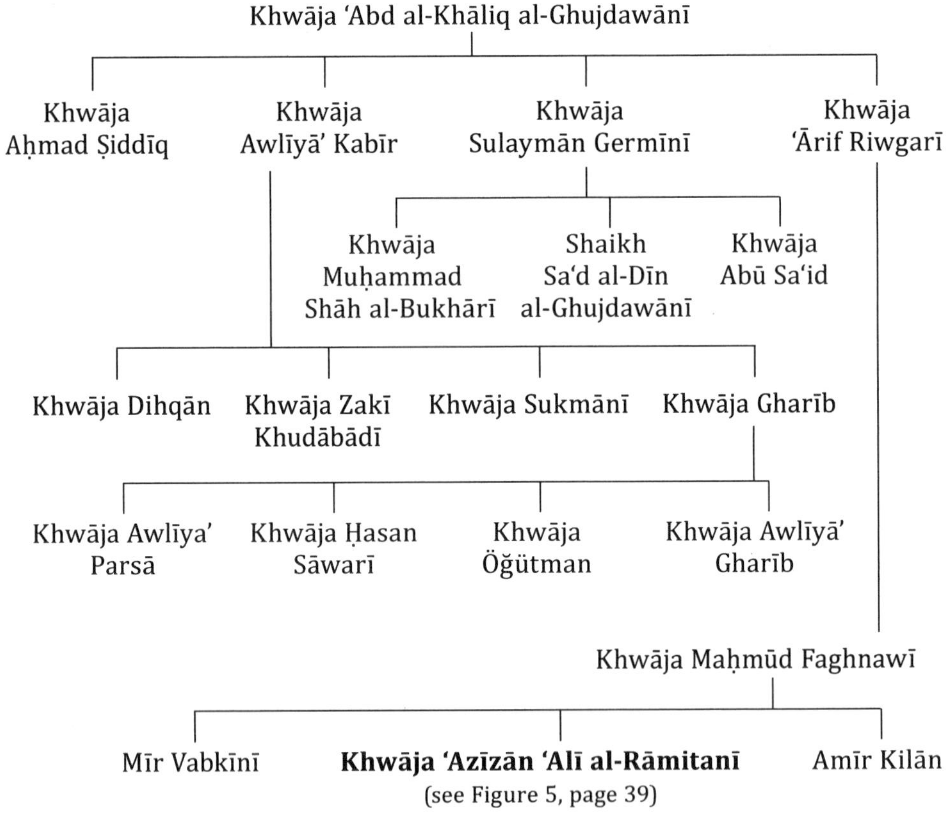

Figure 4

The Deputies of Khwāja ʻAbd al-Khāliq Ghujdawānī

♦ Khwāja Aḥmad Ṣiddīq, First Deputy of Khwāja ʻAbd al-Khāliq Ghujdawānī

Khwāja Aḥmad Ṣiddīq, the first deputy, was from Bukhārā. He took the place of the venerable ʻAbd al-Khāliq when the latter died. Shortly before he himself passed on, he assigned his pupils to Khwāja Awlīyā' Kabīr and Khwāja ʻĀrif Riwgarī, and subsequently "those two great men were active in Bukhārā, inviting seekers to the Truth and providing suitable candidates with training and guidance."

His tomb is said to be situated in the village of Mughyān, some ten miles from Bukhārā.

♦ Khwāja Awlīyā' Kabīr, Second Deputy of Khwāja ʻAbd al-Khāliq Ghujdawānī

Khwāja Awlīyā' Kabīr was also a native of Bukhārā. It was while he was a student there that he happened to meet Khwāja Ghujdawānī one day in the market. He saw that the Khwāja was holding some meat and asked if he could carry it home for him. The venerable Khwāja agreed and invited the young man to stay for supper. After this, Khwāja ʻAbd al-Khāliq "treated him like his own son and initiated him into the teachings of the spiritual path." Khwāja Awlīya' immediately lost interest in his ordinary studies, left his college, and dedicated his life to the service of the venerable 'Abd al-Khāliq.

He is known to have undergone a spiritual retreat of forty days in the mosque at the Gate of the Money-changers in the Bukhārā Bazaar. Khwāja 'Ubaidallāh al-Aḥrar was very pleased with him on this account and made no secret of his admiration. He is recorded as saying: "The retreat from distractions is not just a matter of keeping out absolutely all inconsequential thoughts. You could say that its purpose is to prevent any distraction whatsoever from disturbing one's inner collectedness. It is like trying to keep sticks and straws on the surface of a stream from entering the water."

His tomb is in Bukhārā. He had four deputies, the first of whom was Khwāja Dihqān. He stepped into his Master's teaching role on the death of Khwāja Awlīyā'. His tomb is in the vicinity of Bukhārā.

His second deputy was Khwāja Zakī Khudābādī, while the third was Khwāja Sukmānī, whose tomb is beside the resting place of Khwāja Awlīyā'. The fourth deputy of Khwāja Awlīyā' al-Kabīr was his son, Khwāja Gharīb, who succeeded his father after Khwāja Sukmānī. He was a contemporary of Saif al-Dīn Bāhirzī, one of the chief companions of Shaikh Najm al-Dīn al-Kubrā. The two of them were often in each other's company. It was around this time that Shaikh Ḥasan al-Bulghārī came to Bukhārā "from the lands of the Russians and Bulgars." This celebrated shaikh was well known for his attractive good humor. During the three years he spent in Bukhārā, he became closely acquainted with Khwāja Gharīb. In fact, he would never leave his presence.

Tradition has it that Shaikh Ḥasan al-Bulghārī would say: "In the course of my life, I have sat at the feet of many saints and mystics, but I never met anyone equal to Khwāja Gharīb."

Khwāja Gharīb had four deputies: Khwāja Awlīyā' Parsā, Khwāja Ḥasan Sāwarī, Khwāja Öğütman, and Khwāja Awlīyā' Gharīb. All four lie buried in Bukhārā and its environs.

♦ Khwāja Sulaymān Germīnī, Third Deputy of Khwāja 'Abd al-Khāliq Ghujdawānī

Khwāja Sulaymān Germīnī, third deputy of Khwāja 'Abd al-Khāliq Ghujdawānī, is also affiliated to Khwāja Awlīyā' Kabīr, under whom he served. He was once asked to explain the meaning of the Prophetic Tradition: "The sincere are in grave peril" (*al-mukhiliṣūna 'alā khaṭrin 'aẓīm*). This was his reply: "The station occupied by those who are sincere is very elevated and they must therefore be fearful lest they fall. The 'grave peril' goes with the loftiness of their station. The closer we approach the sun, the more we are affected by its heat."*

His tomb is situated in the small town of Germīn, nearly forty miles beyond Bukhārā. His deputies were Khwāja Muḥammad Shāh al-Bukhārī, Shaikh Sa'd al-Dīn al-Ghujdawānī, and Khawaja Abū Sa'īd.

♦ Khwāja 'Ārif Riwgarī, Fourth Deputy of Khwāja 'Abd al-Khāliq Ghujdawānī

Khwāja 'Ārif Riwgarī, fourth deputy of Khwāja 'Abd al-Khāliq Ghujdawānī, was born near Bukhārā in the village of Riwgir, where his tomb is to be found. The chain of transmission from Khwāja Bahā' al-Dīn Naqshband goes back through Khwāja Riwgarī to end with Khwāja Ghujdawānī.

♦ Khwāja Maḥmūd Faghnawī, Successor of Khwāja 'Ārif Riwgarī

Khwāja Maḥmūd Faghnawī was the distinguished deputy and successor of Khwāja 'Ārif Riwgarī. He was born in the village of Faghnī, in the district of Iknī, six or seven miles from Bukhārā. His tomb is in the same place. He made his living as a carpenter in Iknī. He was the first in the line of the Masters of Wisdom to introduce "public dhikr in accordance with the needs of the time and as required by the

---

**Rashaḥāt*.

condition of the seekers." When asked the reason for this innovation he responded by saying: "Let sleepers awake!"

His first deputy was Mīr Vabkīnī, who had a deputy called Khwāja 'Alī Ergundānī. The *Thamarāt al-Fu'ād* also mentions another deputy of Khwāja Faghnawī by the name of Amīr Kilān.

Khwāja 'Azīzān 'Alī al-Rāmitanī

One of the Greatest of the Masters of Wisdom

Figure 5

Khwāja 'Azīzān 'Alī al-Rāmitanī is the second deputy of Khwāja Maḥmūd Faghnawī, whom he succeeded, and one of the greatest of the Masters of Wisdom. He is said to have been endowed with high spiritual qualities and remarkable charismatic powers. Born in Rāmitan, a large township some six miles from Bukhārā, he practiced a weaver's trade. Mawlānā 'Abd al-Raḥmān Jāmī says this about him in *Nafaḥāt al-Uns:* "I have heard from some of the great that the venerable Mevlânâ Jalāl al-Dīn Rūmī was alluding to him when he wrote: 'If inner state [*ḥāl*] did not carry more weight than speech [*qāl*], would the notables of Bukhārā have become the slaves of Khwāja Nassāj?'"*

Three questions were put to Khwāja 'Azīzān by a contemporary of his called Rukn al-Dīn 'Alā' al-Dawla Samnānī:

QUESTION: Like you, we also serve the passing guest. Your hospitality is not equal to ours, yet people approve of you and find fault with us. What is the explanation?

ANSWER: Plenty of people do service as a favor, but very few consider it a favor to be allowed to serve. Strive to feel gratitude for the opportunity to serve, till nobody complains about you any more.

QUESTION: We have heard it said that you received your training directly from Khiḍr, on him be peace. What about that?

ANSWER: There are true lovers among the servants of God, Glorified and Exalted is He, and Khiḍr is their lover.

QUESTION: We hear that you do your dhikr in an audible voice. What kind of dhikr is that?

ANSWER: And we hear that you do your dhikr secretly: since we have got to hear of it, it is just as if you also did it aloud.

Mawlānā Saif al-Dīn, a well-known religious scholar of the time, also asked Khwāja 'Azīzān why he practiced audible dhikr. He replied: "There is a noble Tradition, accepted by all the scholars, to the effect that in the throes of death it is permissible to breathe one's last by pronouncing the testimony of faith in a loud voice. For the dervish, every breath is his last."

Shaikh Badr al-Dīn Maidānī, a close friend of Shaikh Ḥasan al-Bulghārī, asked him: "In compliance with the divine command, we

---

**Nassāj* is the Arabic word for "weaver."

remember God constantly. Should remembrance be a verbal dhikr or dhikr from the heart?" Khwāja 'Azīzān replied: "It begins as remembrance from the tongue and ends with remembrance from the heart."

In answer to the question: "What is faith?" he used the language of his trade, saying, "It is the warp and the woof."

Among his other sayings are these:

> Watch yourself in two activities: speaking and eating.
>
> If a son of Khwāja 'Abd al-Khāliq had been alive at that time, Ḥusain ibn Manṣūr al-Ḥallāj would not have gone to the gallows, for he would have trained the cotton-carder* and saved him from that fate.
>
> Pray with lips you have not employed in sin.

Rukn al-Dīn Nūrī, another prominent shaikh and scholar, once asked him: "Why is it that on the day-before-time-began some of the souls answered 'Yes' to the question: 'Am I not Your Lord?,' while on the Day of Resurrection no one will reply to the divine enquiry: 'Whose is the Sovereignty today?'" Khwāja 'Azīzān replied:

> The day-before-time-began was the day for imposing sacred legal obligations. Speech is appropriate in matters of sacred law. But the Day of Resurrection is the day when obligations are removed and the World of Reality is inaugurated. In the presence of Reality words are out of place. That is why God, Exalted is He, will give His own answer on that day saying: "It belongs to Allāh, the Unique and Irresistible."†

Many miracles are attributed to him. In manner and speech he displayed a free and open disposition and was clearly a man of sharp and independent wit. He is said to have lived to the age of 130. His mausoleum is in Khwārizm. He used to visit the poor and needy. Khwāja

*Literal meaning of the name *Ḥallāj* in Arabic.
†*Rashaḥāt.*

Muḥammad, the elder of his two sons, was eighty years old when his father died. The younger son was Khwāja Ibrāhīm.

When Khwāja 'Azīzān was near the end of his earthly life, he authorized his younger son to continue his teaching work. When his friends asked him why he had not chosen his elder son, who was a learned and perfected person, as his successor, he said: "Khwāja Muḥammad is not long for this world and must very soon rejoin me."

The venerable Khwāja 'Azīzān died on 28 Dhū-l Qa'da in the year 721/1321 and Khwāja Khurd Muḥammad followed him nineteen days later, on 17 Dhū-l Ḥijja. According to another tradition, the date was 715/1315. The *Rashaḥāt* sets the date of Khwāja Ibrāhīm's death in the year 793/1390.

Apart from his two sons, Khwāja Rāmitanī had four well-known deputies: Khwāja Muḥammad Kulāhdūz, Khwāja Muḥammad Ḥallāj Balkhī, Khwāja Muḥammad Bāwardī, and Khwāja Muḥammad Baba Sammāsī.

♦ Khwāja Muḥammad Baba Sammāsī

According to the *Rashaḥāt,* "He was the most excellent companion of the venerable 'Azīzān and a man of outstanding spiritual development." His birthplace was the village of Sammās in the vicinity of Rāmitan some ten miles from Bukhārā. His place of burial is the same village. "It is related that when the venerable 'Azīzān was close to death, he chose Khwāja Muḥammad Baba, from all his friends and companions, to be his deputy and successor, instructing them all to follow and serve him."

There is a well-known story, recounted in the *Rashaḥāt*, that every time Khwāja Baba Sammāsī passed through the village of Qaṣr-i Hinduwān, which was to be the birthplace of the venerable Bahā' al-Dīn Naqshband, he would say to his companions: "The land hereabouts gives off the scent of a hero." On one such occasion he said: "The smell has got stronger, that hero must have been born." In fact, Khwāja Bahā' al-Dīn Naqshband had come into this world three days previously.

In accordance with a local custom, Bahā' al-Dīn's grandfather placed a gift on the child's breast and asked Baba Sammāsī to give him his blessing. The venerable Khwāja said: "This is my son and we have accepted him." Turning to his companions, he said: "This is the very hero whose scent we noticed. Before long, this child will become the paragon of the age and the stalwart helper of the people of Love!" He then turned to Sayyid Amīr Kulāl, who would be his successor, and said: "Do not refuse to undertake the training of my son Bahā' al-Dīn, and be sure to treat him kindly. If you are negligent in this, I shall not forgive you." The venerable Amīr rose to his feet and vowed, with his hand on his heart: "I am no man if I fail you."

According to Khwāja 'Ubaidallāh al-Aḥrar, Muḥammad Baba had a small orchard in the village of Sammās, which he would sometimes prune himself. But whenever he cut a twig a spiritual state would overwhelm him, the knife would fall from his hand and he would spend some time sitting on a stump, lost to this world.

His four deputies were: Khwāja Ṣūfī, Khwāja Muḥammad Sammāsī (his son), Mawlānā Dānishmend 'Alī, and Sayyid Amīr Kulāl.

♦ Sayyid Amīr Kulāl

A descendant of the blessed Prophet, he was the greatest of Khwāja Muḥammad Baba Sammāsī's successors. He was born and buried in the village of Sukhārī, about seven miles from Bukhārā. He was a potter by trade, as his nickname Kulāl indicates in the dialect of Bukhārā. His father, Sayyid Ḥamza, gave this name to his second son also.

According to the *Rashaḥāt*, "His lady mother said: 'While I was carrying the Amīr in my womb, I would get a stomach ache every time I ate dubious food. When this had happened several times, I realized it was caused by the baby. Seeing this miracle, I became very wary of what I ate and my hopes were raised.'"

In his youth, Sayyid Amīr was a keen wrestler. One day as he was wrestling in a match, Muḥammad Baba Sammāsī happened to come by. He stopped to watch the sport and said to his companions: "In that ring I see a champion whose spiritual teaching will bring many people to completion." Sayyid Amīr caught the Khwāja's eye and was immediately attracted to him. He abandoned the wrestling match and followed Khwāja Muḥammad home. He was accepted as a pupil and initiated in the spiritual path.

Sayyid Kulāl served Baba Sammāsī for twenty years:

> Twice every week, on Mondays and Thursdays, he used to travel from Sukhārī to Sammās to sit at the Khwāja's feet. It was quite a ride, since the distance between the two places is nearly twenty miles. Under the direction of Baba Sammāsī, he proved an exceptional disciple in the Way of the Masters, eventually attaining the stage of perfection and becoming a teacher in his own right.*

He had four sons and four deputies, all of them men of mature and enlightened spirituality. His sons were: Amīr Burhān, Amīr Ḥamza (d. 880), Amīr Shāh, and Amir 'Umar.

His deputies were: Khwāja Bahā' al-Dīn Naqshband, Mawlānā 'Ārif Dikkarānī, Shaikh Yādigār Gunsarūnī, and Khwāja Jamāl al-Dīn Dehistānī.

His sons and deputies trained their own companions and deputies in their turn. Also numbered among the well-known companions of Amīr Kulāl were: 'Alā' al-Dīn Gunsarūnī, Amīr Kilān Wāshī, Shaikh Badr al-Dīn Maidānī, and Shaikh Sulaymān Germīnī, to name but a few.

Outstanding above all the rest of the deputies trained by Sayyid Amīr Kulāl are the venerable Bahā' al-Dīn Naqshband and Mawlānā 'Ārif Dikkarānī. For several years after the death of Amīr Kulāl, Khwāja Bahā' al-Dīn served Mawlānā 'Arif with loyal affection. The spiritual maturity of the latter is apparent in the sayings attributed to him. When people brought him gifts, Mawlānā would decline to accept them, saying: "It is appropriate to accept a gift when one is blessed with the influence to help the giver get what he wants. We do not possess that influence."

**Rashaḥāt*.

When he sensed that his death was approaching, Mawlānā 'Ārif sent an urgent summons to Khwāja Bahā' al-Dīn, who hastened to Bukhārā from Merv—where he was meeting friends after returning from his first Pilgrimage to Mecca. In the village of Dikkarān, Mawlānā 'Ārif commended Khwāja Muḥammad Parsā to him and said:

> As you know, there is a total unity between us. We have spent many loving moments together. Now my inevitable time has come. I have studied my companions and yours and I consider Khwāja Muḥammad Parsā to have the greatest spiritual capacity and humility. Whatever I have acquired on this path, I commit it all to your charge. Do not neglect it.

Three days after giving this advice he left this world, and Khwāja Bahā' al-Dīn attended personally to his funeral arrangements before returning to Merv.

Khwāja Muḥammad Bahā' al-Dīn 'Shah' Naqshband and His Contemporaries

Eponymic of the Naqshbandiyya and a remarkable figure even among the Sufis of Turkestan, Khwāja Muḥammad Bahā' al-Dīn Naqshband was one of those complete and truly original characters who emerge at intervals separated by long periods of time. He inherited the mantle of Muḥammad, on him be peace. His personal name was Muḥammad ibn Muḥammad al-Bukhārī. He was born in the month of Muḥarram 718/1318, not far from Bukhārā in the village of Qaṣr-i Hinduwān, which had changed its name to Qaṣr-i 'Ārifān by the time of his death on the third night of Rabī' al-awwal 791/1389. His mausoleum is in the same village. According to the *Risâle-i Bahâ'iyye,* the venerable Naqshband was a well-built man of medium height. His beard was grey, tending more to white than to black. His features were round, his cheeks ruddy, his brows widely spaced, his moustaches clipped, and his eyes a dark chestnut color.

Although, like the venerable Uwais, he had the aptitude for spontaneous, individual development; he derived grace from the spiritual influence of Khwāja 'Abd al-Khāliq Ghujdawānī; he received the blessing of Muḥammad Baba Sammāsī when he was only three days old, and he was initiated and trained by Sayyid Amīr Kulāl.

When he was still a child, his features already showed the marks of spiritual authority and nobility, and his charismatic powers were apparent. According to his biography, his progress on the path began with the visions he saw one night, when he received guidance and direction from the spiritual emanation of 'Abd al-Khāliq Ghujdawānī. This is how he describes the experience:

> I was shown three lamps. Then I saw a high throne, in front of which a green curtain was stretched. A throng surrounded the throne and amid that throng was Khwāja Muḥammad Baba Sammāsī. I realized that these people were departed Masters of Wisdom.
>
> One of those present informed me that the venerable 'Abd al-Khāliq Ghujdawānī was seated upon the throne, while the others were deputies: Khwāja Aḥmad Ṣiddīq, Khwāja Awlīyā' Kilān, Khwāja 'Ārif Riwgarī, Khwāja Maḥmūd Faghnawī, and Khwāja 'Azīzān 'Alī Rāmitanī.
>
> Pointing to Muḥammad Baba, my guide said: "You will come to know this man as your shaikh. You have been given the charismatic power to ward off imminent disaster."
>
> I then heard a voice from the throng crying out to me: "Listen carefully! The venerable Khwāja will tell you things of great importance to you in the way of Truth." I asked permission to see the venerable Khwāja and offer my salutation. The curtain before me was raised and I saw a luminous saint. He accepted my salutation and then gave me instruction concerning the beginning, middle, and end of the spiritual path. He congratulated me on my aptitude, which was confirmed by the three lamps I had first seen, and told me to discover the Mysteries by putting my talents to good use.
>
> He then went on to stress the following advice: "Whatever happens, always follow the path marked out by divine command and prohibition. Keep a firm resolve and never abandon the Prophetic example and the practice of good works. Steer clear of heretical innovations, take the Traditions of the blessed Muḥammad Muṣṭafā for your guide and make a profound study of all that has been recorded about God's Messenger and his Companions."
>
> After this counsel had been offered, they all advised me to go to Nasaf and enter the service of Sayyid Amīr Kulāl.*

**Nafaḥāt* and *Rashaḥāt.*

It was subsequent to these events that Khwāja Naqshband met Sayyid Kulāl in Nasaf. "The venerable Amīr treated me with great kindness and favor and taught me the dhikr, which he made me practise silently as a way of developing the habit of negation (of selfish promptings) and of affirmation (of conscience).*

As recounted in the *Rashaḥāt,* seeing Bahā' al-Dīn's sincerity and integrity, Amīr Kulāl began to treat him with special attention and favor. This aroused the jealousy of certain other pupils, some of whom complained that Bahā' al-Dīn performed his dhikr in silence instead of chanting it aloud with the rest. Some time later, Amīr Kulāl was engaged with five hundred of his followers in the building of a mosque and meeting hall. At a convenient moment he remarked to those who had voiced complaints: "You have not understood my son Bahā' al-Dīn. He enjoys the special care of God, Exalted is He, who protects and envelops his whole being. The favor of God's servants is a consequence of the Exalted One's favor, so my special attention to him is involuntary."

> After a while, Bahā' al-Dīn was summoned by the Khwāja, as he was busy carrying sun-dried bricks. Addressing him in front of all his followers, he said: "Bahā' al-Dīn my son, I have looked after you in fulfilment of the dying wish of Khwāja Muḥammad Baba Sammāsī. I have trained you as I promised, for he told me to prepare you with the utmost care to be a teacher in your own right. This I have now accomplished." He then pointed to his blessed breast as he said: "I have nourished you with all I had to offer, and now the bird of your spiritual prowess is ready to leave the nest. Your influence for good will soar like a royal falcon. Henceforth, you are fully qualified. Whenever the scent of wisdom reaches your nostrils, follow that scent with all the dedication your high calling demands."
>
> Khwāja Bahā' al-Dīn said: "This blast from the venerable Amīr was the cause of all my tribulations. Had I walked steadily in the

*Nafaḥāt.

venerable Amīr's footsteps, I would have been safely out of harm's way."*

After this, Khwāja Naqshband entered the service of Amīr Kulāl's second deputy, Mawlānā 'Ārif Dikkarānī, with whom he continued for seven years beyond the death of Sayyid Kulāl:

> During this period he behaved toward Mawlānā 'Ārif with the utmost deference. He would keep a respectful distance if they happened to be performing their ablutions together, and would never walk in front if they were going somewhere. He was always a perfectly obedient companion as he recognized that Mawlānā 'Ārif had been his senior in the service of Amīr Kulāl, who had been his teacher for many years previously.†

Shortly before Amīr Kulāl died, he instructed his companions to follow Khwāja Bahā' al-Dīn. When his pupils and friends protested on the grounds that Khwāja Bahā' al-Dīn had not practiced public dhikr, the Amīr said: "In all his actions he is guided by the Exalted Truth and not by his own will."

Khwāja Bahā' al-Dīn Naqshband said:

> A special awareness arose in me when I began to practice silent dhikr. That was the secret I sought. Mawlānā 'Arif and I spent thirty years together looking for the people of Truth. We went twice on Pilgrimage together. Our wanderings took us to many corners and retreats in search of people we had heard about. Had I been able to find anyone else remotely resembling Mawlānā 'Ārif in spiritual development, I would not have come to this part of the world. Try to imagine someone, to sit close to whom is better than being in Paradise!

*True individuals are inexorably doomed to face tribulation and affliction along the spiritual path. By no other means can they attain the stations of ultimate liberation. The individual way is a way of great hardship.

†*Rashaḥāt.*

Following the death of Mawlānā 'Ārif, Khwāja Bahā' al-Dīn Naqshband acted upon the advice he had received from Sayyid Kulāl and spent three months in the service of Qāsim Shaikh, the Yasavī. Qāsim Shaikh received him well, saying: "I have nine sons already, you make the tenth and are more pleasing to me than all the rest."

In later years the venerable Naqshband would welcome Qāsim Shaikh with great reverence whenever he came to Bukhārā. The shaikh said he had never met anyone as earnestly devoted to the quest as Bahā' al-Dīn Naqshband.*

After his time with Qāsim Shaikh, he received in a dream that he should attach himself to Khalīl Ata, one of the great Turkish shaikhs, in whose service he remained for twelve years.

♦ Khalīl Ata, Eminent Turkish Shaikh

Khalīl Ata was one of the most eminent Turkish shaikhs. According to the *Nafaḥāt,* Khwāja Naqshband had dreamt on first entering the Sufi path that he was assigned to a dervish named Khalīl Ata. The features of this dervish remained in his memory, and he described them to his mother. That great and pious lady told her son that he was destined to meet a Turkish shaikh.

The venerable Naqshband was constantly on the lookout for this shaikh, until, as he tells us (in the *Nafaḥāt*):

> I came across him in the Bukhārā Bazaar. I recognized him the moment I saw him and learned that his name was Khalīl. To my great regret, I was not granted the opportunity, at that time, of sitting and conversing with him. I returned home and that same evening a messenger came to say: "That dervish Khalīl wants to see you." As it was summertime, I took him some fruit. As soon as I saw him I asked if I might tell him my dream. Speaking in Turkish, he said: "What does that matter now that we are face to face?" I was drawn to him

**Nafaḥāt.*

more strongly than ever and I had many wonderful and extraordinary experiences in his company.

Some time after this, Khalīl Ata succeeded to the throne of Transoxiana, and Khwāja Bahā' al-Dīn remained in his service throughout the six years of his rule. Bahā' al-Dīn tells us (in the *Nafaḥāt*): "He treated me with great affection. Sometimes gently and sometimes sternly, he taught me how to conduct myself as a good servant. I derived great benefit from this and was enabled to make great strides in the spiritual path."

Khalīl Ata once remarked to his courtiers in the hearing of the venerable Khwāja: "Anyone who serves me for the sake of God, Exalted is He, will attain eminence among the people." He repeated this several times. "I understood what he was driving at," said Khwāja Bahā' al-Dīn.

After six years the sultanate collapsed, and all that pomp and circumstance was scattered to the winds. The venerable Khwāja now lost all interest in worldly affairs and went to Bukhārā, where he settled in the nearby village of Rīwdan.

♦ Mawlānā Bahā' al-Dīn Qishlāqī and Mawlānā 'Ārif Dikkarānī

Khwāja Naqshband also sat at the feet of Mawlānā Qishlāqī, the father-in-law of Mawlānā Dikkarānī. With him he studied Prophetic Tradition. Mawlānā 'Ārif Dikkarānī had been a pupil of his father-in-law, Bahā' al-Dīn Qishlāqī, before entering the service of Amīr Kulāl. It was through this connection that Mawlānā 'Ārif and Khwāja Naqshband first met. This meeting took place at the winter palace (*qishlāq*) of Sultan Mubārak Shāh where Bahā' al-Dīn Qishlāqī had been born.*

Mawlānā Bahā' al-Dīn Qishlāqī was considered to be "the paragon, leader and guide of his contemporaries." He was a master of exoteric

*Approximately forty miles from Bukhārā.

and esoteric learning and was said to possess remarkable psychic talents.

When Khwāja Naqshband first met Mawlānā Qishlāqī, the latter said to him: "You are such a high-flying bird that only 'Ārif Dikkarānī is fit to be your friend and companion." This filled Khwāja Naqshband with a longing to meet Mawlānā 'Ārif. Bahā' al-Dīn Qishlāqī sensed what he was feeling, so he went up to the roof of the house and called out: "'Ārif, 'Ārif, 'Ārif!" At that moment, 'Ārif Dikkarānī was sowing cotton seed in a village over sixty miles away,* but he received the message. Setting out in haste at midday, he reached the winter palace in time to meet Naqshband at supper that very evening.

According to Khwāja 'Ubaidallāh Aḥrār: "Mawlānā Qishlāqī was a great man and Khwāja Naqshband sat at his feet." He seems to have had the same person in mind when he said to his disciples: "There are certain supremely illustrious individuals who serve with sincere and complete devotion and manifest perfect humility. Though you may not be capable of matching them, you should at least be aware of their existence."

♦ Pilgrimage and Passing of Khwāja Bahā' al-Dīn Naqshband

Khwāja Bahā' al-Dlī Naqshband went twice on the Pilgrimage to Mecca. On the second journey he was accompanied by Khwāja Muḥammad Parsā. When they reached Khurāsān he sent Muḥammad Parsā and his other followers ahead to Nīshāpūr while he went to Herāt to see Mawlānā Zain al-Dīn Tā'ibadī, with whom he stayed for three days. He then rejoined his party at Nīshāpūr, and they continued their journey to Arabia. After his return from the Pilgrimage he spent some time in Merv and eventually came to Bukhārā, where he stayed till the end of his days.

We have various accounts of his death at the age of seventy-four (seventy-one, according to the Western calendar). The great Mawlānā

*In those days, a two-day journey.

Muḥammad Miskīn relates that Khwāja Naqshband went to the funeral, in Bukhārā, of a shaikh called Nūr al-Dīn al-Khalwatī. Friends and relatives of the deceased were weeping and wailing in mourning, and some of those present objected to this, considering it unseemly and un-Islamic behavior. Everyone had a different opinion on this subject, so the venerable Khwāja said: "When my life ends, I shall show the dervishes the proper way to die."

"These words stuck in my memory," said Mawlānā Miskīn, "and I recalled them when the venerable Khwāja entered his death sickness and was carried to his room in the caravanserai to await the end. His principal companions came there to visit him every day and the Khwāja treated each of them with great kindness. As he was breathing his last, he raised his hands in prayer, made a long supplication, then drew his hands over his face and finally surrendered his spirit."

One of his deputies, 'Alā' al-Dīn Ghujdawānī, was by him when he died. "When I entered his noble presence," said he, "the Khwāja was in the throes of death. He recognized me and said: 'Pull up the table and eat, 'Alā'.' I took a few mouthfuls, trying to be obedient, but it was a great effort since I had completely lost my appetite. Then I pushed the table aside."*

Some of those present were wondering who would be left in charge of his teaching work. The venerable Khwāja picked up their thoughts and said: "Why do you annoy me at a time like this? That matter is out of my hands. The decision rests with God, Exalted is He. He will confer that honor as and when He wills."

Khwāja 'Alī Dāmād relates:

> During his final sickness, the venerable Khwāja commanded me to dig his grave. I entered his presence after performing this task and I found myself wondering who would be designated as his successor in the teaching work. Suddenly, he raised his blessed head, saying: "It is just as I said when we were going on Pilgrimage. If anyone wishes

---

***Rashaḥāt.*

for me, let him look to Muḥammad Parsā." Two days later he passed on into the presence of God.*

♦ Sayings of the Venerable Khwāja Naqshband

From the *Nafaḥāt*:

> Our method is to work through friendly intercourse. Seclusion fosters repute, with all its attendant dangers. Welfare lies in association. Those who follow this way derive great benefit and blessing from gathering together in a friendly spirit.
>
> We are not granted access to the mystery of ultimate union. The secret of true wisdom is difficult, though not impossible, to attain.†

From the *Rashaḥāt*:

> We do not accept everyone and if we do accept it is with difficulty. The conditions of acceptance are hard to fulfil. Sometimes a capable pupil presents himself but there is no Master fit to receive him. Sometimes the Master is ready but qualified pupils are not to be found. (Said in connection with his initiation of Ya'qūb Charkhī.)
>
> There are two kinds of science. One is the science of the heart, which is the useful knowledge taught by the Prophets and Messengers. The other is verbal science, which is proof to mankind of the Exalted Truth.

From the *Risâle-i Bahâ'iyye*:

> It was from a gambler that I learned steadfast devotion in the quest for Truth. This man lost everything in the gambling den and his companion advised him to give it up, but he said: "Ah my friend, I

**Rashaḥāt.*

†Ultimate union is unattainable since it would mean identification of the Godhead and the created universe—a monistic or pantheistic view. As for the secret of true wisdom, this is the stage of ultimate reality, accessible only through divine grace to those who inherit the mantle of Muḥammad, on him be peace. The venerable Naqshband was one of these rare and consummate beings.

couldn't stop playing this game if I knew it would cost me my head." When I heard this, my heart was filled with an enthusiasm that still fuels my endeavor.

At the outset of my spiritual quest, my state was such that I would always lend an ear if I saw a couple of people in conversation. If their discussion was of God, I felt blissful; if they were talking about anything else, I felt sad and heavy at heart.

In my youth, I prayed: "O Lord, grant me the strength to bear the burden of this way, so that I may accomplish whatever strenuous tasks await me." This supplication of mine was accepted, for now that I am a Master I find myself relieved of austere and ascetic disciplines.

As a novice, I followed the advice of Khwāja Baba Sammāsī and took many courses in Prophetic Tradition and Islamic studies. But what helped me most along the path was abasement and humiliation. I was led in through that gate and whatever I may have acquired, that is how I came by it.

It is a mighty task to practise self-denial and abnegation. For us on this path, these qualities represent the end of a lifeline, which can lead us safely to our goal. I was admitted by the gate of self-effacement and humble supplication, the starting-point from which I reached whatever I may have attained.

I am featureless and colorless from twenty years under the spiritual influence of Khwāja Muḥammad al-Tirmidhī. Should anyone wish to recognize me now, I am still colorless and featureless.

We are the means whereby the seeker can reach his goal. The seeker must be detached from us in order that he may achieve that goal.

One day in the village mosque at Zīvertūn (or Rīwdan), I was sitting with my back against a pillar and my face toward the *qibla*. A sudden ecstasy flooded my whole being. I was taken out of myself entirely and I heard a voice say: "Know that you have attained your goal!"

Acts of worship confer being, for being is what we seek through our worship.

The venerable Shaikh Abū-l Ḥasan al-Kharaqānī used to say: "The way that leads from God to man is all beatitude within beatitude, while the way from man to God is all error within error." That is why the seeker needs the company of a spiritual guide, for he cannot otherwise be sure of keeping to the straight path.

It seems we are accused of pride. Our pride is no ordinary pride, but spiritual exaltation.

If we have any achievement to our name, we owe it to our habit of poverty.

What do the Sufis mean by saying: "The poor man has no need of God"? They are referring to genuine poverty, which is the station of total contentment.*

As for the Prophetic Tradition, "perfect poverty is Allāh," this is said to refer to that complete annihilation of the self, the experience of which is accompanied by the manifestation of the Divine Essence.

On my way from Bukhārā to Nasaf one day, as I was going to see Sayyid Amīr Kulāl, I happened to meet a man on horseback. I declined his pressing invitation to keep him company. When I reached my destination, Sayyid Kulāl said: "That was the venerable Khiḍr, why did you not accept his kind offer?"—"I was bound for your noble presence," I replied, "and my association with you enables me to dispense with the company of Khiḍr."

If a person really knows the divinity of the Truth with complete familiarity, that person will know all other things by mystical revelation. No reality will remain concealed from him, for all things and all

---

*In genuine and perfect poverty, contentment with God is so complete that the very thought of Him is redundant.

objects of knowledge are but the external appearance of the attributes and names of God, Exalted is He.

Nothing that exists is as vast as the heart of one who knows God. Heaven and earth are a mere jot by comparison. That is why our Lord and Maker said: "I could not fit into My earth and My heaven, yet I found room in the heart of My believing servant."

All hearts have equal capacity, but the extent of the wisdom they contain is far from uniform.

If I noticed the faults in my friends, I would not have a friend in the world. For a faultless friend is nowhere to be found. Everyone loves good people. What takes skill is winning the game of friendship with bad people.

"What is the goal of the spiritual quest?" asked a famous scholar. "True wisdom in practice," said the venerable Khwāja. "And what is that?" the learned man enquired. "There are things to be believed because they come down to us from a reliable source, though in summary form. Practical wisdom discloses these things in detail, by the test of direct experience."

As Junaid al-Baghdādī said: "Where scholars have failed, Sufis have reached the goal." A scholar in this context is one who concerns himself with names, while the Sufi is one whose concern is with the Named—the reality behind the names.

♦ Some Remarkable Episodes in the Life of Khwāja Naqshband

These episodes in the life of Khwāja Naqshband are culled from the same works as the sayings given above:

Once when the venerable Khwāja Bahā' al-Dīn was in Sarakhs, the king of Herāt sent him a letter of invitation, which read: "We ardently desire the honor of conversing with the venerable Khwāja. What signal does he give?" As he set off for Herāt in response to this invitation, he remarked: "We are under no obligation to meet with kings and sultans, but if we don't go to him, he will come to us, to the discomfort of the dervishes and at great expense to the people."

At the king's court, Bahā' al-Dīn was received with the utmost respect by all the nobles and notables, scholars and shaikhs. But Khwāja Naqshband was a rigorous abstainer from all food of dubious provenance and purity, so he would not eat a morsel at table. Even when they offered him fresh game, slaughtered in accordance with the precepts of Islamic law, he refused to touch it. For all their entreaties, he would not accept a single mouthful.

The Khwāja gave answers to various questions posed by the king:

Q. Is the character of a dervish something you acquired by inheritance?
A. No, it is not an inheritance but a vocation. I was honored to receive such a blessing.

Q. Is solitary retreat one of the techniques you practise?
A. "Solitude in the crowd" is the term used in the teachings of the venerable Khwāja 'Abd al-Khāliq Ghujdawānī, one of the great men of our path.

Q. What is meant by "solitude in the crowd"?
A. It means being outwardly with people but inwardly with God.

Q. Is it humanly possible to achieve this?
A. Had it not been possible, Allāh would not have spoke in the Qur'ān of "men whom neither business nor trade can distract from the remembrance of God" [24: 37].

Q. Some shaikhs maintain that Sainthood is superior to Prophethood. What kind of a Saint could be superior to a Prophet?
A. This refers to the saintliness of the Prophets themselves, for a

Prophet is distinguished by his saintly nature even more than by his religious mission.

After this conversation, the venerable Khwāja left the court and went to stay at the guest house of 'Abdallāh al-Anṣārī. He would not accept a single present from among the precious gifts sent to him by the king. "In all these years," he said, "thanks to the providence of God, Exalted is He, no one has been able to exploit me through my poverty." The king then sent him a shirt, a handkerchief, and a pair of baggy trousers. These he had bought with money he had personally earned and were therefore untainted by any illegality. Surely the Khwāja would accept these small tokens? But still he refused, even though at that time he did not possess one shirt, his turban was in rags, and his shoes were ancient.

If the venerable Naqshband received a visitor when he himself was fasting (outside the month of Ramaḍān), he would immediately provide a meal for the guest, breaking his fast in order to join him at table. One day a dervish of his refused to eat with a guest, even when pressed to do so, on the grounds that he was keeping a supererogatory fast. Turning to his other pupils, the Khwāja said: "That man is far from God. Keep your distance from him."

He once said that whenever Abū Yazīd al-Bisṭāmī re-emerged from the realm of rapturous contemplation, he used to ask after all his friends and companions.

One day the venerable Khwāja was riding along on horseback, while many of his dervishes and friends accompanied him on foot. He wept so much that his followers were also moved to tears, though without knowing why. At length he explained: "I am inwardly such a worthless failure that I do not deserve to have anyone accept my salutation. However, the Exalted Lord has put me to shame by making people take notice of me. None of them knew what I was like inside."

He regarded ascetic practices and especially fasting as the basis of spiritual progress. He used to say: "Without the self-discipline of hunger, thirst, strenuous tasks, and ritual prayer, no one gains mystic insight and vision."

"The aspirant," he said, "should attach no importance to his dreams. He should not occupy his mind with dream experiences, be they subjective or objective. The majority of dreams are produced by false illusions and imaginings, while some stem from worldly attachments. A few are divinely inspired. None of them are of any benefit to the seeker's progress. Certain shaikhs value them, however, as a means of training novices."

When telling how he came to join Sayyid Amīr Kulāl, he said: "The venerable Sayyid Amīr instructed me in 'negation and affirmation,' using the method of Khwāja 'Azizān 'Alī al-Rāmitanī. I concentrated on this and on controlled breathing, giving up the practice of public dhikr. I also obeyed the commands of Khwāja 'Abd al-Khāliq, which sometimes came to me in my dreams, and so I gradually achieved results."

His entire life was devoted to the pursuit and propagation of divine reality and truth. Of the deputies and followers he left behind him, the most famous are: Khwāja Muḥammad Parsā, Khwāja Musāfir Khwārizmī, Mawlānā Muḥammad Figanzī, Mawlānā Ya'qūb Charkhī, Khwāja 'Alā' al-Dīn Ghujdawānī, Mawlānā Saif al-Dīn Mannārī, Shaikh 'Abdallāh Khujandī, Shaikh Sirāj al-Dīn Kulāl Pīrmesī, and, above all, his chief deputy Khwāja 'Alā' al-Dīn 'Aṭṭār.

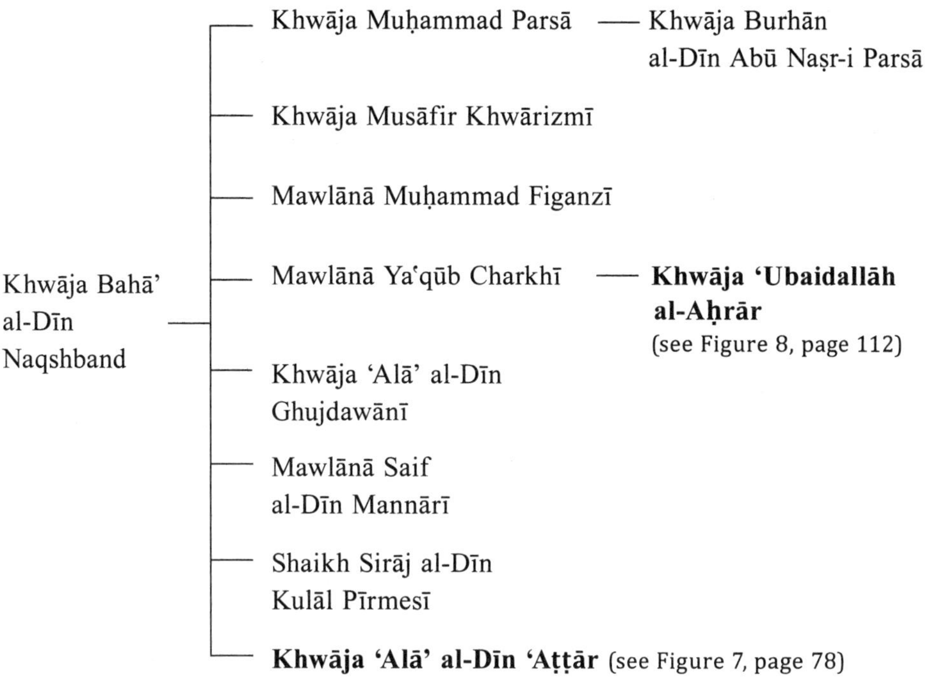
Khwāja Bahā' al-Dīn Naqshband
Khwāja Muḥammad Parsā
Khwāja Burhān al-Dīn Abū Naṣr-i Parsā
Khwāja Musāfir Khwārizmī
Mawlānā Muḥammad Figanzī
Mawlānā Ya'qūb Charkhī
Khwāja 'Ubaidallāh al-Aḥrār
(see Figure 8, page 112)
Khwāja 'Alā' al-Dīn Ghujdawānī
Mawlānā Saif al-Dīn Mannārī
Shaikh Sirāj al-Dīn Kulāl Pīrmesī
Khwāja 'Alā' al-Dīn 'Aṭṭār (see Figure 7, page 78)

Figure 6

Seven of the Major Deputies of Khwāja Bahā' al-Dīn Naqshband

♦ Khwāja Muḥammad Parsā

Khwāja Muḥammad Parsā was the second deputy of Khwāja Naqshband. His personal name was Muḥammad ibn Maḥmūd al-Ḥāfiẓ al-Bukhārī. *Parsā* (the Persian word for "pious") stuck to him as a nickname after Khwāja Bahā' al-Dīn had teased him with it. He must have been born around 750 for he was seventy-three when he died in the year 822/1419. His tomb is in Medina beside the mausoleum of the venerable 'Abbās.

When Bahā' al-Dīn Naqshband fell sick on the way to the Pilgrimage, he said to Khwāja Muḥammad Parsā: "Whatever I may have received as an undeserved gift from the Masters of Wisdom, and whatever I may have acquired through my efforts on this path, I give it all to you, just as Mawlānā 'Ārif, our brother in the Hereafter, gave what he had to me. You must accept this as a trust on behalf of the creatures of the Exalted Truth." Muḥammad Parsā humbly agreed.

Back in Bukhārā after the Pilgrimage, Khwāja Naqshband kept repeating: "All that I have is now yours." He devoted more care and attention to Muḥammad Parsā with every day that passed. Then one day he said: "The spiritual secret I promised you will surely emerge. We are only awaiting the removal of a black rock that is blocking the way." This was his way of saying that the promise would be fulfilled when he had left his physical body; that is, at his death. "The spiritual dominions of the great saints are like the kingdoms of this world. The physical body is an impediment to the perfect man, who is the focal point of reality.*

Khwāja Aḥrār relates: "I heard that Khwāja Bahā' al-Dīn was referring to Khwāja Muḥammad Parsā when he said: 'The purpose of my existence is the emergence of Muḥammad.'" The venerable 'Ubaidallāh al-Aḥrar added: "This ambiguous statement is a veiled hint." Khwāja Naqshband treated Muḥammad Parsā with great favor and kindness. The *Rashaḥāt* and *Nafaḥāt* ascribe charismatic gifts to Muḥammad Parsā. He wrote a number of books, including a well-known work on Sufism called *Faṣl al-Khiṭāb.*

Some of his sayings:

> The curtain between man and God is a tapestry of worldly patterns embroidered on the heart. This tapestry spreads over the heart as a man indulges in idle conversation and admires colorful and shapely forms. It develops still further through the reading of books and the hearing and making of speeches. When a man looks at beautiful pictures or listens to music, this tapestry begins to vibrate with movement. All this results in worldliness and remoteness from the Exalted Truth. The seeker must reject such things. He must avoid everything that fuels the imagination, turning with a pure heart toward God, Exalted is He. It is not the divine custom to allow spiritual progress without trial and tribulation. This state does not arise unless one renounces pleasure and desires.†

> This world bears no relation to the world of the Hereafter. This world is like a poppy seed dropped in a boundless desert.

He went twice on Pilgrimage. The first of these journeys was made in the company of Khwāja Bahā' al-Dīn Naqshband, whose final Pilgrimage it was. Muḥammad Parsā made his second Pilgrimage in

---

**Rashaḥāt.*

†*Rashaḥāt.*

Muharram 822, thirty years after the death of Khwāja Baha' al-Dīn. In that year he set out with his followers in a caravan from Bukhārā. They reached Mecca by the Nīshāpūr road, passing through Nasaf, Tirmidh, Balkh, and Herāt. In all the places they passed, they were accorded great honor and respect by the local sayyids, shaikhs, and scholars, dignitaries and common folk. They visited the tombs of saints along their route.

Mawlānā 'Abd al-Raḥmān Jāmī said:

> As I recall, it was in the month of Jumādā-l'ūlā or at the beginning of Jumādā-l'ākhira that he passed through the province of Jām in the course of this pilgrim journey. My father had gone to greet him, along with a great crowd of supplicants and devout people. I was just five years old at the time. At a sign from my father, someone picked me up and held me in front of Muḥammad Parsā as he sat on his camel. The Khwāja was kind to me and gave me a bulb of the Kirmānī plant.
>
> For sixty years I have retained in my mind's eye the joyful vision of his illuminated countenance, and I have preserved in my heart the delight of that blessed meeting. To his blessing and favor I owe the bond of sincerity and conviction, love and affection that ties me to the Masters of Wisdom. By virtue of that bond, I hope to be resurrected in the company of the sincere and loving followers of those venerable Masters.*

After Khwāja Parsā had performed the rites and ceremonies of the Pilgrimage, he became sick and made his farewell circumambulation in a litter before leaving Mecca for Medina. Arriving there on Wednesday, 23 Jumādā-l'ākhira 822, he visited the Prophet's resting place and "received blessings of many kinds from the noble Messenger, on him be peace." On Thursday, the twenty-fourth, he died there in Medina.

**Nafaḥat.*

The people of Medina joined those of his caravan for his funeral prayers, which were also attended by the Ottoman scholar Mawlānā Shams al-Dīn Fanārī (Molla Fenâri), who was also making Pilgrimage at the same time. He was interred that Friday evening near the mausoleum of the venerable 'Abbās.

Shaikh Zain al-Dīn Khwāfī had a white stone slab sent from Egypt for his tomb. "Because of that stone his noble tomb still stands out from the rest."*

♦ Khwāja Burhān al-Dīn Abū Naṣr-i Parsā

Also called the Greatest Khwāja, Khwāja Abū Naṣr-i Parsā was the son and deputy of Khwāja Muḥammad Parsā. Mawlānā Jāmī mentions in the *Nafaḥāt* that he was at the same level as his father in religious law and Sufism, but surpassed him in "self-abnegation and generosity."

He concealed his spirituality with such masterly skill that no one would ever have thought him a Master of Wisdom. If a question was put to him, he would feign ignorance, saying: "Let's look it up in the book." When he opened the book it was always either at or very near the page where the answer to the problem could be found.

One day in a meeting, mention was made of the works of the venerable Muḥyī-l Dīn ibn al-'Arabī. The Khwāja quoted these words of his father, Khwāja Muḥammad Parsā: "The *Fuṣūṣ* is the soul and the *Futūḥāt* is the heart. The urge to follow the blessed Messenger becomes firm and strong in one who truly knows and understands the *Fuṣūṣ*."

He died in the year 865/1460 and lies buried in Balkh.

♦ Khwāja Musāfir Khwārizmī

He was in the service of Khwāja Naqshband and later in that of Khwāja Parsā. Khwāja 'Ubaidallāh was often in his company.

A native of Khwārizm, he lived beyond the age of ninety and enjoyed the friendship of many great teachers. He relates how he and

**Rashaḥāt.*

some of his dervishes once held a session of sacred music and dance (*samā*‘) in the presence of the venerable Naqshband, who said: "We do not practise this ourselves, but we do not deny its validity."

Khwāja Musāfir also relates:

> One day Khwāja Bahā' al-Dīn was engaged in some construction work. His companions were working hard and Muḥammad Parsā was also busy mixing plaster. In the midday heat, the venerable Khwāja gave them a break and each of them found a shady spot in which to sleep. Muḥammad Parsā lay with his muddy feet stretched out in the sun. The venerable Naqshband walked around looking at them all, until he came up to Khwāja Muḥammad Parsā. Seeing him sleeping in this condition, he rubbed his face on one of those muddy feet and said: "My God, have mercy on Bahā' al-Dīn, in honor of this foot!"

♦ Mawlānā Muḥammad Figanzī

A close friend and companion of Khwāja Naqshband, he was born in Figanz between Bukhārā and Samarqand. He spent a long time in the service of Muḥammad Parsā after the death of the venerable Naqshband, whom he had joined in his youth.

As he himself relates:

> It would often happen that the venerable Khwāja Muḥammad Parsā left the mosque after the night prayers and stood at the threshold, leaning on his staff while exchanging a few words with his followers. He would then fall silent and in that silence become "absent" from himself. His mystic absence would last until the muezzin gave the call to morning prayer, when the Khwāja would go back into the mosque to pray.

Khwāja ‘Ubaidallāh al-Aḥrār said that this spiritual state was often witnessed in the line of the Masters and that it was acquired through dhikr, austerity, and self-discipline.

♦ Mawlānā Ya'qūb Charkhī

One of the chief disciples of Bahā' al-Dīn Naqshband, he was the spiritual teacher of Khwāja 'Ubaidallāh al-Aḥrār (see page 92). Born in Charkh, a village near Ghazna, he died in Khuluftu near Ḥiṣār, and there he lies buried. He had a great liking and affection for Khwāja Naqshband even before joining him as a pupil.

He studied the exoteric sciences for a long time in Herāt and Bukhārā, as well as in Egypt, where he and Zain al-Dīn Khwāfī were fellow students of Mawlānā Shihāb al-Dīn Shirwānī, one of the greatest scholars of the time.

He was on his way home, after completing his studies in Bukhārā, when he happened to meet Khwāja Bahā' al-Dīn. "Keep me in your heart," he pleaded. The venerable Khwāja said: "Will you join me later?" The conversation then continued:

"I long to enter your service."

"Why?"

"You are a great man, respected by all the people."

"Give me a better reason than that!"

"As the blessed Prophet said: 'If God, Exalted is He, makes someone his friend, He sows affection for that person in the hearts of His other creatures.'"

The Khwāja smiled at this and said: "We are among God's loved ones." Charkhī was amazed, for he now recalled a dream he had had a month before. In that dream he had been told: "Become a disciple of God's loved ones!" He again asked the Khwāja for his blessing, then took his leave of him.

At Khwāja Bahā' al-Dīn's suggestion, he traveled home by way of Balkh, meeting with Tāj al-Dīn en route. It was not long, however, before something brought him back to Bukhārā, where he entered the service of the venerable Naqshband.

After years of spiritual training, Ya'qūb Charkhī was given permission to leave Bukhārā. Khwāja Naqshband said to him: "Whatever has been transmitted from us to you concerning the spiritual path and the secrets of reality, that you must now convey to the servants of God, Exalted is He, so that you may be the cause of their felicity."

After Khwāja Naqshband's death, he followed his instructions and went to Chigāniyān to join Khwāja 'Alā' al-Dīn 'Aṭṭār, from whose company he never parted until this Master also died. Three days after Khwāja 'Alā' al-Dīn's death, Mawlānā Ya'qūb Charkhī returned to Khuluftu, where he eventually ended his days.

♦ Khwāja 'Alā' al-Dīn Ghujdawānī

Khwāja 'Alā' al-Dīn Ghujdawānī was a disciple of Khwāja Naqshband, who handed him on to Muḥammad Parsā. According to the *Nafaḥat*, "A charming talker, he used to experience complete rapture. He would sometimes become lost to himself in the middle of speaking."

Khwāja Muḥammad Parsā took Khwāja 'Alā' al-Dīn along with him when he went on Pilgrimage. Khwāja 'Alā' al-Dīn was by then quite old and weak. The dervishes appealed to Muḥammad Parsā to excuse him from the journey, asking why he needed to take him along. Khwāja Muḥammad replied: "The sight of 'Alā' al-Dīn reminds me of the kinship of the saints and this is a great help and support to me."

At the age of sixteen, he was introduced to the spiritual path through the guidance of Kilān Wāshī, one of the deputies of Amīr Kulāl. According to 'Ubaidallāh Aḥrār, he spent his youth in the service of Khwāja Baha' al-Dīn Naqshband until that Master died. The rest of his life was spent in the company of Khwāja Muḥammad Parsā and his son Abū Naṣr-i Parsā, both of whom acknowledged the benefit of Khwāja 'Alā' al-Dīn's companionship.

Khwāja Aḥrār used to say: "One sees few seekers with such an appetite for Sufi wisdom and reality as Khwāja 'Alā' al-Dīn. He was like an example of how to follow the spiritual path."

At the death of Khwāja 'Alā' al-Dīn, Khwāja Abū Naṣr-i Parsā preached a sermon in which he said: "Khwāja 'Alā' al-Dīn was a shelter for us all. We were safe and comfortable in his care and protection.

Now that he has attained God's mercy, we need to be cautious and apprehensive."*

Khwāja Muḥammad Parsā was a frequent visitor of Baba Shaikh Mubārak. One day Khwāja 'Alā' al-Dīn Ghujdawānī badly wanted to go along with him on one of these visits, but Khwāja Muḥammad Parsā said: "You may not come. You would expect to find in the company of Baba Shaikh Mubārak what you used to get from the noble sessions of Khwāja Bahā' al-Dīn Naqshband, but you will not recover that same taste and are therefore bound to lose confidence in Shaikh Mubārak. That is why it is not appropriate for you to come along."

♦ Mawlānā Saif al-Dīn Mannārī

A companion of Khwāja Bahā' al-Dīn Naqshband, he was well versed in exoteric and esoteric knowledge alike. The venerable Naqshband took a great interest in him. He remained in the Khwāja's service until that Master's death, after which he joined Khwāja 'Alā' al-Dīn 'Aṭṭār.

♦ Shaikh Sirāj al-Dīn Kulāl Pīrmesī

He first attached himself to Amīr Ḥamza, the son of Amīr Kulāl, and then became a follower of the companions of Khwāja Bahā' al-Dīn Naqshband. While in the service of Amīr Ḥamza he practiced many austerities and strenuous spiritual exercises. At one point he entered a state of rapturous contemplation in which he remained outwardly unconscious for three days and nights. Hearing of this, Amīr Ḥamza told another novice to whisper in his ear: "Amir Hamza says you are to come back out of there." Sirāj al-Dīn immediately showed signs of sensation and movement and soon recovered consciousness.

He was a potter by trade. There was always a pleasant atmosphere at the meetings he conducted; they had a great appeal, and many attended them regularly. The venerable Sa'd al-Dīn Kāshgharī was often in his company.

**Rashaḥāt.*

Khwāja 'Alā' al-Dīn 'Aṭṭār

Foremost Deputy of Khwāja Bahā' al-Dīn Naqshband

Khwāja 'Alā' al-Dīn 'Aṭṭār was the son-in-law of Khwāja Bahā' al-Dīn Naqshband and "the most outstanding and accomplished of his deputies and companions." His personal name was Muḥammad 'Alā' al-Dīn ibn Muḥammad al-Bukhārī. A native of Khwārizm, he was the spiritual teacher of Sayyid Sharif al-Jurjānī.

The venerable Khwāja (Naqshband) used to assign most of his pupils to him, saying: "Alā' al-Dīn has lightened my load considerably." The light of sainthood and the signs of charisma were manifest in him in the most complete and perfect degree. Through the blessing of his company and the excellence of his instruction many seekers made great progress and reached the more advanced stages of spiritual perfection.*

His father, Muḥammad al-Bukhārī, had two other sons, called Khwāja Mubārak and Shihāb al-Dīn. When his father died, 'Alā' al-Dīn did not take an inheritance but devoted himself to his studies at one of the colleges of Bukhārā. His true talents were recognized by Khwāja Bahā' al-Dīn Naqshband, who came one day and took 'Alā' al-Dīn from his simple cell in the college. Despite 'Alā' al-Dīn's humble and self-effacing protestations, he made him his son-in-law. Then he deliberately sent him, barefoot and carrying a tray on his head, to sell apples

**Nafaḥāt* and *Rashaḥāt*.

in the streets and bazaars of Bukhārā, hawking his wares "at the top of his voice," especially in front of the shop belonging to "that honest pair," his two brothers. After this he initiated him in the spiritual path.

According to the biography of Khwāja Naqshband, the Khwāja made 'Ala' al-Dīn sit beside him during meetings and from time to time would turn toward him. When some of his intimates asked the reason for this, he said: "When I remind myself of him, it is as if I had seen the House of Allāh."

Khwāja 'Aṭṭār himself relates:

> At the time when I first became a disciple of the venerable Khwāja Bahā' al-Dīn, I was speaking about the heart to a certain Sufi at Rāmitin. When I said I did not know the true nature of the heart, this person said: "In my opinion the heart is like the moon when it is three days old." I mentioned this to the venerable Khwāja, who was standing up at that moment. He placed his blessed foot on mine, whereupon I experienced a great exaltation and witnessed the entire universe within myself. When I returned to my ordinary state, he said: "That is the heart, not what that dervish said. How can you comprehend the nature of the heart unless you have witnessed its true greatness? To know the heart is to know one's purpose, and to find the heart is to find one's purpose."

A debate arose among the religious scholars of Bukhārā, some of whom affirmed and some of whom denied the possibility of seeing God, Glorified and Exalted is He. Having great confidence in Khwāja 'Alā' al-Dīn 'Aṭṭār, the scholars asked him to be their umpire.

To those who inclined to the Mu'tazilite doctrine and denied such vision, the venerable Khwāja said: "Come and sit in our company for three days in a row, in perfect ritual purity and in silence, then let us give a verdict."

The scholars complied with these conditions. "At the end of the third day they were overwhelmed by an ecstasy so unbearable that they collapsed and started rolling on the floor. When they recovered themselves they got up and confessed in perfect humility: 'We have come to believe that the vision of God is true.'" From that time on they never left the Khwāja's company.

As Khwāja Aḥrar relates, Muḥammad Parsā often experienced ecstasy during his contemplation and spiritual communion. In 'Alā' al-Dīn 'Aṭṭār, on the other hand, conscious presence and awareness predominated. "The Masters of Truth and Reality consider conscious awareness and sobriety more complete and perfect than ecstasy and rapturous inebriation." That is why all Khwāja Baha' al-Dīn's disciples took the oath of allegiance to Khwāja 'Aṭṭār after Naqshband's death, including Muḥammad Parsā, to whom he had assigned them before he died.

♦ Sayings of Khwāja 'Aṭṭār

Khwāja Muḥammad Parsā wrote down some of Khwāja 'Aṭṭar's sayings, intending to add them as an appendix to the biography of Bahā' al-Dīn Naqshband, but this proved impossible. Here are a few of these sayings, taken from his manuscript notes:

> The purpose of asceticism is to repudiate material and physical attachments and to turn oneself in the direction of the real, spiritual world.
>
> It is most necessary for the novice to bind his heart to the guide. Since the spiritual guide and director is the mirror of divine reality, communion with him leads the pupil to annihilation and ecstasy. Genuine renunciation cannot be achieved without ecstasy. The novice must therefore remain attached to his spiritual director during the early stages of his quest, until he achieves the ecstasy that causes one to renounce everything but God. Otherwise, he will fall by the wayside and fail to experience annihilation.
>
> The advanced traveller no longer needs this bond, for he has achieved the reality of final renunciation. For him, everything has become the mirror of absolute beauty. To reach the essence of being

is to see oneself as a drop in the ocean, an atom in the sun. For those who have reached this stage, it is limited and inadequate to see the absolute beauty in the mirror of the spiritual guide.

The object of the quest is to rid oneself of all attachments that stand in the way of the Truth. Our revered Khwāja Bahā' al-Dīn was most careful never to regard any object or state as belonging to him. If he donned a new robe, he would wear it as something borrowed, saying: "This is so-and-so's robe."

When the material and spiritual worlds are both erased from the seeker's eyes, annihilation has been achieved. When the traveller's own being is hidden from him, that is annihilation within annihilation.

The seeker's main obstacle is his own being. What prevents anyone from attaining universal knowledge is his inability to transcend his own partial knowledge, just as the obstacle to universal vision is the inability to transcend one's individual and partial vision.

One needs a guide endowed with the spirit of Muhammmad, for by giving one's heart to him, and annihilating one's own being in his, one may reach the final stage of annihilation and so attain the ultimate goal of the quest.

Real knowledge must be treated with care and respect. As the venerable Muḥyī-l Dīn ibn al-'Arabī explains in the *Futūḥāt,* "to unite ideas with faith" demands an exceptional degree of skill and wisdom, such as only pure saints possess.

The great shaikhs say that success belongs to those who strive. The teacher can only help the pupil to the extent of the latter's diligence in obeying his instructions. The spiritual guide may devote his attention to the disciple and the effect will be noticeable for several days, "but it is not permanent." In the company of the venerable Khwāja Bahā' al-Dīn, we spent all our time on the development of self-discipline. Yet I saw few dervishes go through even one whole day with sustained effort.

A spiritual state will sometimes arise in the pupil during his contemplation or work, only to disappear again almost at once. The aspirant should not be dismayed by this, for with steadfastness and application these spontaneous experiences will acquire stability and permanence. The seeker may even develop such skill as to be able to achieve annihilation and "annihilation of annihilation" of his own volition.

Visiting the tombs of great saints can be a useful source of spiritual blessing, depending on the extent of the visitor's understanding and the quality of his meditation. While great benefit can be derived from physical closeness to sanctified tombs, physical distance is no obstacle in reality to the contemplation of holy spirits.

If anyone enters this path by way of imitation he will certainly achieve realization. Khwāja Naqshband instructed me to imitate him. I certainly achieved positive results whenever I did so.

Ecstasy rather than self-possession is the characteristic mark of this fraternity. As Shaikh Muḥyī-l Dīn ibn al-'Arabī, sanctified be his secret, said: "According to the majority of shaikhs, ecstasy is an imperfect stage. In our view however, ecstasy is the most perfect and most excellent of all stages."

If the aspirant finds his progress blocked, the fault lies with him and is not due to any lack of divine grace. When the seeker has removed these obstacles by the diligent and assiduous practice of spiritual exercises, a rapturous state will arise through the spiritual influence of the teacher and that pupil's prayer will be the supplication of the noble Muṣṭafā: "O Lord, increase my rapture and my immersion in You."

Will and volition are of great benefit to mankind, for everyone encounters obstacles and difficulties. By force of will and sustained effort those obstacles can be surmounted. Will and volition are very influential in general, in happiness and misery, in our ups and downs.

[Just as his outer qibla is the direction of Mecca], the seeker's inner qibla should be God's Pure Essence; the eye of his heart should never deviate from this direction; God should be his only aim in both worlds and he should sacrifice his all for the sake of the Truth.

When they asked Manṣur al-Ḥallāj to which school of Islamic jurisprudence he belonged, he replied: "I belong to the school of my Lord."

What is required of the faithful aspirant is that his body should keep to the sacred law, his mind and spirit to the mystic path and reality, and his secret soul to "without asking how."

They told one of the Elders he should marry, but he said: "I have not yet reached puberty." A man becomes mature when he achieves sainthood. Until then he is no more than a child.

Our venerable Khwāja Bahā' al-Dīn Naqshband used to say: "A lawful livelihood is nine-tenths of worship. In this age, the most nearly lawful ways of earning a living, after trade, are farming and horticulture."

The desire to be always in the company of men of God is the result of a strong disposition to other-worldliness.

Friendly intercourse is an important part of the example set for us by the blessed Prophet. It is necessary to spend much time in friendly intercourse with this Sufi fraternity and to acquire their habits, both external and internal.

The purpose of delay is to allow time for capacity to develop. What is acquired prematurely is quickly lost, for there is no understanding of its nature and source.

Abandon ceremonies and customs. Whatever is customary among the people, you should do the opposite. The venerable Messenger, on him be peace, was sent to abolish human ceremonies and customs.

♦ Sayings of Khwāja Naqshband Transmitted by Khwāja 'Aṭṭār

Some important sayings transmitted by Khwāja 'Alā' al-Dīn 'Aṭṭār in the biography of Khwāja Naqshband*:

> Khwāja Naqshband said: "Two of us set out on this path. My aim was total renunciation. Having received God's grace, I was enabled to forsake everything and to achieve my aim."
>
> The venerable Bahā' al-Dīn used to say: "True prayer, fasting, spiritual exercises, and self-discipline lead to the presence of the divine oneness, Sanctified and Exalted is He, but in my opinion, the shortest road of all is the 'negation of being.'"
>
> The venerable Naqshband said: "The wise have three and only three means of reaching the truth, namely: vigilance [*murāqaba*], contemplation [*mushāhada*], and examination of conscience [*muḥāsaba*]. 'Vigilance' means not to see the creation because one is constantly looking toward the Creator. 'Contemplation' means witnessing mystical enlightenments received within the heart. 'Examination of Conscience' means not allowing the states we have already achieved to become obstacles in the way of attaining further stations."
>
> The venerable Khwāja Bahā' al-Dīn used to initiate promising seekers into the bliss of this vigilance at the first step. "As he devoted more and more of his noble attention to him, the seeker would be brought to the degree of non-existence and then with still further attention to the stage of annihilation."
>
> Shāh Naqshband said: "We are merely the means to the achievement of Reality. In order to achieve his true goal, the disciple must be cut loose from us. After reaching the stage of annihilation and becoming intimate with the permanence of the Exalted Truth, the traveler

**Maqāmāt-i Muḥammad Bahā' al-Dīn Naqshband.* This work was written on the instructions of Khwāja 'Alā' al-Dīn by his disciple Ṣalāh al-Dīn ibn al-Mubārak.

must renounce everything. This is the station of the perfect spiritual guides who are capable of perfecting others."

Khwāja Naqshband pointed to his own body as he said: "If this poor beggar could find a body in greater ruination than this, he would hide his treasure there."

What is meant by the saying "Metaphor is the bridge to Reality" is that all acts of worship, whether external or internal, verbal or physical, are metaphorical or imitative. Those who tread this path can only attain Reality by performing and transcending these acts of worship.

♦ Last Illness and Final Teachings of Khwāja 'Alā' al-Dīn 'Aṭṭār

Khwāja 'Alā' al-Dīn 'Aṭṭār fell sick on the second day of Rajab 802/1400. For eighteen days he suffered severe pains in the midriff and head before dying after the late evening prayer on Wednesday, 20 Rajab. His tomb is in the village of Nev-Chigāniyān.

The author of the *Rashaḥāt* claims to have seen these notes, in the handwriting of the venerable Khwāja Muḥammad Parsā, recording things said by Khwāja 'Alā' al-Dīn during his last illness:

"If it were in accordance with the gracious will of God, Glorified and Exalted is He, and the grace and favor of Khwāja Bahā' al-Dīn, the whole of mankind would attain the goal of Reality."

"Do not model yourselves on the diverse aspects of my external behavior. Cultivate inner and outer harmony, otherwise you will fall into discord and confusion."

"Friends and dear ones have gone and those who remain will also depart. That world is certainly superior to this one." At this point he turned to a companion, who was speaking highly of a certain orchard he had seen, and said: "The dust (of the tomb) is more beautiful; this world holds no more attraction for me. When friends come looking for me in future, they will go away disappointed."

He then praised Khwāja Muḥammad Parsā lavishly, and to his face, recalling happy memories of days gone by.

Khwāja Muḥammad Parsā also recorded how one of the dervishes saw the venerable 'Alā' al-Dīn in a dream forty days after his death. He said to that dervish: "The favors bestowed on us by God, Glorified and Exalted is He, are far greater than my friends imagined."

His chief companions and deputies were: Khwāja Ḥasan 'Aṭṭār, Mawlānā Ḥusām al-Dīn Parsā al-Balkhī, Mawlānā Abū Sa'īd, Khwāja 'Ubaidallāh al-Iṣfahānī, Shaikh 'Umar al-Bāyazīdī, Khwāja Aḥmad al-Samarqandī, Sayyid Sharīf al-Jurjānī, and Mawlānā Niẓam al-Dīn Khāmūsh.

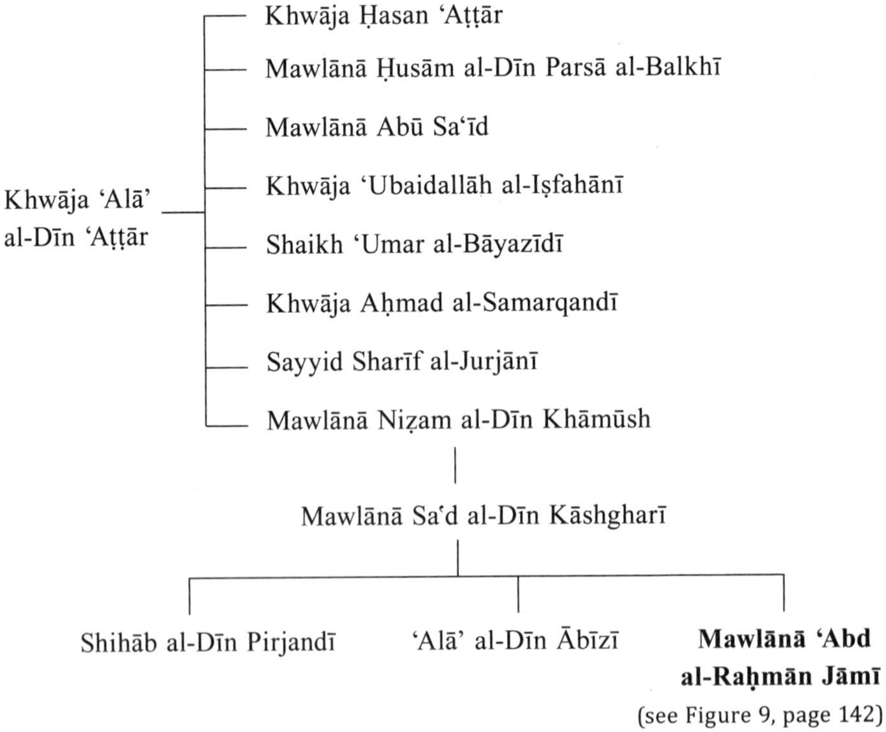

Figure 7

Chief Companions and Deputies of Khwāja 'Alā' al-Dīn 'Aṭṭār

♦ Khwāja Ḥasan 'Aṭṭār

The son of Khwāja 'Alā' al-Dīn, in his childhood he attracted the attention of his grandfather, the venerable Bahā' al-Dīn Naqshband. He received spiritual training from his father. He is said to have possessed a strong faculty for ecstasy, which enabled him to influence whomever he wished. By directing his attention toward people, he could enable them to lose consciousness and attain non-existence. He could induce an experience of absence and annihilation normally accessible only to rare individuals on the spiritual path after prolonged effort and striving. He seems to have been very famous for this in Transoxiana and Khurāsān. Anyone who kissed his hand was sure to establish a bond of affection with him and "to be helped toward the eventual achievement of blissful non-being."

According to the *Nafaḥāt,* when he went out one morning all those on whom his gaze alighted "became intoxicated with the wine of non-existence and experienced ecstasy." The same faculty was observed in some of his disciples.

According to the *Rashaḥāt,* when he was a child he once mounted a calf and rode around while his friends ran alongside. Khwāja Bahā' al-Dīn Naqshband came by and said, when he witnessed the sight: "The day will come when mighty kings will walk in this boy's train."

Many years later, after he had moved to Khurāsān, Khwāja Ḥasan 'Aṭṭar went to visit Sultan Mīrzā Shāhrukh at Bāgh-i Zāghān in Herāt. Mīrzā presented him with a mule. He had helped the Khwāja to mount and was holding the stirrup with one hand and the bridle with the other, when the beast became refractory and started to move off. Mīrzā Shāhrukh was obliged to run a few paces in the Khwāja's train until the mule stopped. Khwāja Ḥasan then dismounted and turned in the direction of Bukhārā while offering a "humble supplication." He told Sultan Shāhrukh the story of what had happened in the time of his grandfather, Khwāja Naqshband.

A dervish of Khwāja Ḥasan 'Aṭṭār was on his way to the Pilgrimage when he broke his journey at Herāt. Signs of ecstasy, unconsciousness, and rapture were apparent in the countenance of the dervish. Whenever he passed through the markets and bazaars "he was clearly so overwhelmed by an influence from within that he was quite unaware of the hustle and bustle around him."

According to Mawlānā 'Abd al-Raḥmān Jāmī, this dervish always kept his attention on the features of the venerable Khwāja Ḥasan 'Aṭṭar and preserved the Khwāja's countenance in the treasury of his heart. "By virtue of this, the ecstatic quality of the venerable Khwāja was infused into that dervish."

We encounter the following ideas in a treatise on the Way of the Masters, which he wrote under the patronage of a sincere and devoted follower, who was one of the great men of that age:

> Know that the method followed by this Order is the highest path, the shortest of the ways that lead to God. For this method consists in removing the veils of individualization from the face of Oneness. By extinction and annihilation, this method completely consumes the entire universe of manifestation.
>
> In reality the ways of this Order begin where those of other

shaikhs come to an end. This Order reaches the boundary of annihilation and its starting point is ecstasy.

Following the customary practice of the Masters of Wisdom, Khwāja Ḥasan 'Aṭṭār would take upon himself the maladies of others. Having reached Shīrāz on his way to the Pilgrimage, he took upon himself the illness of a local nobleman who was one of his disciples. The patient recovered, but the venerable Khwāja died of that disease. His death occurred on the Festival of Sacrifices in the year 826/1423. His body was taken to Nev-Chigāniyān and laid to rest beside his father.

He left a son by the name of Khwāja Yūsuf 'Aṭṭār, as well as many deputies and companions, of whom the most famous was Shaikh 'Abd al-Razzāq. The latter met Sayyid Qāsim Tabrīzī and won his respect and commendation.

His son, Khwāja Yūsuf, corresponded with his contemporary, Shaikh Bahā' al-Dīn 'Umar. According to Khwāja 'Ubaidallāh Aḥrār, it was mentioned one day, during one of Shaikh Bahā' al-Dīn 'Umar's sessions, that certain eminent Sufis considered breath retention essential to the dhikr and had ordered it to be practiced.

It seems that Shaikh 'Umar maintained that breath retention was peculiar to the Indian Orders and that the essential thing in the Way of the Masters was "not breath retention, but breath control."

When this came to the notice of Khwāja Yūsuf 'Aṭṭār, he wrote a letter to Shaikh Bahā' al-Dīn 'Umar, in which he said: "We have heard that you ban breath retention and maintain that no shaikh of this Order ever prescribed it. In fact, breath retention in dhikr was prescribed by the venerable Khwāja Bahā' al-Dīn Naqshband and his deputies. Why do you reject it?"

In reply, Shaikh 'Umar wrote: "It was not our intention to reject their practice." He closed the subject in "vague and general terms."

♦ Mawlānā Ḥusām al-Dīn Parsā al-Balkhī

He was initiated in the service of Khwāja Bahā' al-Dīn Naqshband, on whose instructions he joined Khwāja 'Alā' al-Dīn 'Aṭṭār, achieving a high degree of perfection in his company. He is famous for his strict adherence to the sacred law, his piety, and his constant recitation of litanies and remembrances. Khwāja Aḥrār met him in Balkh. When Khwāja 'Ubaidallāh asked him why advanced travelers in the Way of the Masters were still required to practice dhikr, Mawlānā Ḥusām al-Dīn said that dhikr at the level of final accomplishment was "not for traversing stages but for transcending them."

'Ubaidallāh al-Aḥrar relates that Mawlānā Ḥusām al-Dīn al-Balkhī was very punctual in his work, his gatherings, and his worship, following the example of 'Umar and Zain al-Dīn al-Khwāfī. He used to keep open house for visitors from early morning till the afternoon prayer. From the afternoon prayer till dawn the next day he would have no contact with anyone.

♦ Mawlānā Abū Sa'īd

One of the principal companions of Khwāja 'Alā' al-Dīn 'Aṭṭār, he also served under Khwāja Ḥasan. He met Sayyid Qāsim Tabrīzī in Herāt.

♦ Khwāja 'Ubaidallāh Imām al-Iṣfahānī

According to the *Rashaḥāt,* the following ideas were expressed in a short treatise Khwāja Iṣfahānī wrote under the patronage of a great prince:

> What is called the "heart" is the comprehensive human reality, of which the higher and lower aggregations of the universe are the detailed particulars. This reality, however, is exempt from incarnation. To this one should direct one's eye, one's thought, one's imagination, and all one's faculties, for it is certain that the quality of occultation and non-being will become apparent in that state.
>
> According to what we have heard from the venerable Khwāja Bahā' al-Dīn Naqshband, if our idea of the Truth is pure, denial will only intensify it, for the Truth is untouched by human negation.

Otherwise it would disappear. Also: "the spiritual aim of this order is concentrated on non-existence, the boundary of the Valley of Wonder and station of the manifestation of the lights of the Essence. At this station, being is no more."

Khwāja Iṣfahānī said: "On the day when I first entered his company, the venerable Khwāja 'Alā' al-Dīn 'Aṭṭār recited these verses to me:

'Let no trace of you remain,
In this alone perfection lies.
In Oneness make your being naught,
Union lies in this alone.'"

♦ Shaikh 'Umar al-Bāyazīdī

A follower of Khwāja 'Alā' al-Dīn, he was said to be "the most diligent servant of his spiritual court."

♦ Khwāja Aḥmad al-Samarqandī

Khwāja Aḥmad al-Samarqandī was initiated in the service of Shaikh Zain al-Dīn Khwāfī, from whom he received his diploma. He is one of the most noteworthy personalities in the line of the Masters. It is clear from his recorded sayings and thoughts that he was capable of a high level of abstraction and that his spirit of liberation gave him access to the divine realities.

Because of the affection he felt for the Naqshbandī Masters, he often frequented the company of Khwāja 'Alā' al-Dīn 'Aṭṭār before traveling to Khurāsān, 'Irāq, the Ḥijāz, and Transoxiana. After leaving him to go to Herāt, he used to express his nostalgia in long letters.

Zain al-Dīn Khwāfī authorized and encouraged him to preach in Herāt. At first the shaikh advised the people of Herāt to pay allegiance to Aḥmad Samarqandī. Later, however, Shaikh Zain al-Dīn was alienated from him because he often recited the verses of Sayyid Qāsim Tabrīzī in his preaching. He broke up Dervish Aḥmad's congregation by spreading rumors and even went so far as to call him an unbeliever.

When the venerable Khwāja Aḥrār encountered him in Herāt, Khwāja Aḥmad told him about the abuse he had suffered and turned to him for help. Khwāja 'Ubaidallāh said: "Go and start preaching afresh in such and such a mosque, where your community will be bigger than ever." Aḥmad Samarqandī did, in fact, enjoy greater popularity than before, despite Zain al-Dīn Khwāfī's efforts to undermine it. As a result, the fame of 'Ubaidallāh Aḥrār spread among the people and he acquired the reputation of having conquered Shaikh Zain al-Dīn.

Khwāja 'Ubaidallāh said: "Aḥmad Samarqandī's audience should have included Abū Ḥafs al-Ḥaddād, Shaikh Abū-l Qāsim Jurjānī, Junaid al-Baghdādī, and Abū Bakr al-Shiblī, if the lofty truths he uttered were to be understood."

In his preaching one day, Khwāja Samarqandī was speaking of lofty and subtle truths, when certain negative people in the congregation objected: "What is the use of saying things that nobody can understand?" He responded by saying: "If you cannot understand the words of this Order, how are you able to judge that all those present are as incompetent as yourselves?"

According to the author of the *Rashaḥāt,* the following passages were discovered in a collected work, written—in Arabic—in Khwāja Aḥmad's own hand:

> In the Holy City of Jerusalem, I turned myself toward the All-Holy One. I heard Him saying: "Worship Me!" I asked: "O Lord, how should I worship You?" Came the reply: "Devote yourself to Me entirely, emptying your soul of all that is other than Me."
>
> When I was in the City of Dervishes, I heard a spiritual being addressing me in spiritual language while I was awake. The voice said: "This bodily form you call your own person is nothing of the sort." From this I understood that our limited being is not, as some

suppose, the same as Absolute Being. I knew through enlightenment that the Being of the Creator is exempt from comparison with the being of creation. He is a Light that spreads throughout the universe, the entirety of which is like a mere atom in the radiance of that Light. As an atom arises from the light of the sun and becomes visible by that light, so does the whole universe become manifest and exist by the Light of the Real Sun.

This humble creature was graced with the experience of an ascension and abstraction. This ascension was in the Essence of the Exalted Truth, that is, it was an illumination of the Divine Essence. In that abstraction and heavenly ascension, this was shown to be the difference between the Essence of God and the essence of this humble creature: God's Essence is without end, but the essence of this humble wretch is finite.

I saw Khwāja 'Abdallāh al-Anṣārī in a dream. He said: "The relationship between us is that of father and son, there is no 'you and I' in it."

After these observations, Khwāja "Dervish" Aḥmad Samarqandī had written the following stanzas in Persian:

Love am I, my whereabouts in space and time unknown;
Phoenix of the West am I, my mark and aim unknown.
With eyebrow and with dimple I shoot my human game:
These are my bow and arrow, but that remains
unknown.

Although from every atom I shine forth like the sun,
The purpose of my shining forth still remains unknown.
I hear with every ear and speak with every tongue,
But strangely enough my tongue and ear remain
unknown.

According to the *Nafaḥat,* "Dervish Aḥmad Samarqandī was a notable disciple and deputy of Zain al-Dīn Khwāfī. He knew the sayings of the Sufis and used them to good effect in his sermons. He also occupied himself with studying and expounding the *Fuṣūṣ*."

'Mawlānā Jāmī noticed the following observations, written in Aḥmad Samarqandī's hand at the end of a copy of the *Fuṣūṣ:*

> The venerable Messenger has indicated to me that I should expound the *Fuṣūṣ al-Ḥikam*. In answer to my question, he commanded me to believe what Muḥyī-l Dīn ibn al-'Arabī wrote about Pharaoh. I then asked: "O Messenger of Allāh, what do you say about Being?" To this he replied: "Do you not see that Being is eternal in the Eternal and phenomenal in the phenomenal?" He then added: "You are both Worshipped and worshipper [*anta ilāhun wa-anta ma'lūhun*], for on the one hand, you are the point of manifestation of the divine attributes, while on the other hand, you have the nature of a limited and individualized creature."

♦ Sayyid Sharīf al-Jurjānī

A favorite companion of Khwāja 'Alā' al-Dīn 'Aṭṭār, Sayyid Sharīf al-Jurjānī occupies an important position in the science of Sufism, being famous as the author of two works entitled "The Unicity of Being" (*Waḥdat al-wujūd*) and "Definitions" (*Ta'rīfāt*). One of the great Sufis of the ninth Islamic century, he died in 824/1421.

Mawlānā Jāmī writes in the *Nafaḥāt:*

> I heard from one of the saints that Sayyid Sharīf al-Jurjānī, who was a master of the subtleties of truth and reality, became a disciple of the venerable 'Alā' al-Dīn 'Aṭṭār and, through his perfect humility and devotion, achieved the highest stages of development in his service. He would sometimes say: "I had no understanding of the Exalted Truth until I joined the company of Khwāja 'Alā' al-Dīn 'Aṭṭār."

On the instructions of Khwāja 'Alā' al-Dīn, Sayyid Sharīf al-Jurjānī became closely attached to Mawlānā Niẓām al-Dīn Khāmūsh. At the end of his lessons he would go and sit quietly at the feet of the venerable Niẓām al-Dīn. As he was sitting one day in this meditative state, an experience of non-being came upon him. His turban fell to the floor and the venerable Niẓām al-Dīn Khāmūsh got up and set it on his head. When Sayyid Sharīf recovered consciousness, he said in reply to a question from the venerable Niẓām al-Dīn: "It has been my lifelong wish that the patterns of knowledge should be erased for a moment from the slate of my perception and that my heart should be relieved of the anxiety of learning. Now, through the grace of your noble company that wish has been granted."*

♦ Mawlānā Niẓam al-Dīn Khāmūsh

He was a prominent disciple of Khwāja 'Alā' al-Dīn 'Aṭṭār and the spiritual director of the venerable Sa'd al-Dīn Kāshgharī. He lived to the age of ninety. It was during his early education that he encountered Khwāja 'Alā' al-Dīn at a meeting held by one of the scholars of Bukhārā.

According to Khwāja 'Ubaidallāh al-Aḥrār, Mawlānā Niẓam al-Dīn said:

> Before entering the service of Khwāja 'Alā' al-Dīn, I used to practise rigorous spiritual exercises and self-discipline. As a result of these exercises, I had many extraordinary experiences. The locked door of a mosque would open for me when I made a sign to the lock. When I heard that Khwāja 'Alā' al-Dīn 'Aṭṭār had come to Samarqand, I felt an intense desire to meet him. I went in search of him and had the honor of meeting first Mawlānā Abū Sa'īd and eventually Khwāja 'Alā' al-Dīn himself. They both told me the time had come to go beyond ascetic practices. I understood what they meant and seized the opportunity to serve Khwāja Aṭṭār, praise be to Allāh.

**Rashaḥāt.*

Mawlānā Niẓam al-Dīn is said to have possessed a peculiar talent for acting as a mirror, in which those who entered his presence saw their own inner state reflected. If his visitor happened to be a man whose religious outlook was legalistic, Niẓām al-Dīn Khāmūsh would speak spontaneously of piety and righteousness. If his guest showed signs of rapture, he would also display enthusiasm and affection. If the caller was of an egocentric and heretical disposition, Mawlānā Khāmūsh would show signs of discomposure and would say: "Your *nisba** got here before you."

Khwāja 'Ubaidallāh al-Aḥrār relates: "Mawlānā Niẓam al-Dīn had strong telekinetic powers. One day he was very distressed to hear of a certain person's shameful conduct. He drew a line on the wall and that person immediately died." According to the *Nafaḥāt* and *Rashaḥāt,* he frequently displayed such powers.

Mawlānā Niẓām al-Dīn used to say that silence is more profitable than talking. Every utterance gives rise to a manifestation of the lower self. Although the emanation of divine grace is incessant, such egotistic manifestations are an obstacle to its reception. One ought to guard one's heart against such manifestations when in the company of saints, for they would sense them and be pained.

♦ Mawlānā Sa'd al-Dīn Kāshgharī

He was the deputy of Khwāja Niẓām al-Dīn and the spiritual teacher of Mawlānā Jāmī. As a young student he read most of the books then available. He was wealthy, but once he had decided to embark on the Sufi path, he entered the service of Mawlānā Niẓām al-Dīn with complete

*The *Rashaḥāt* supplies this note of explanation: "The Masters of Wisdom use the term *nisba* (literally 'relationship') for a person's individual stamp and disposition. According to these Masters, all beings and substances in the entire universe are merely concrete manifestations of the Divine Names. As Muḥyī-l Dīn ibn al-'Arabī put it: 'Substances have not smelled the scent of Being.' In other words, they do not exist of themselves but are intrinsically non-existent. It follows, therefore, that whatever substance and attributes individualized beings may possess, they must be relative [*nisbī*] and not intrinsic. That is why they refer to a person's method and disposition as his nisba."

abandon and renunciation and remained for many long years in his service and company.

Having set out on the Pilgrimage with Khwāja Khāmūsh's permission, he stopped in Khurāsān and met in Herāt with such prominent sages of the time as Sayyid Qāsim Tabrīzī, Abū Yazīd Pūrānī, Shaikh Zain al-Dīn Khwāfī, and Shaikh Bahā' al-Dīn 'Umar.

Of Sayyid Qāsim Tabrīzī, he is reported to have said: "He is the vortex of the spiritual world; united in him are the realities of all the saints of this age." Of Bahā' al-Dīn 'Umar he said: "His mirror faces the Essence and nothing but the Essence does he behold."

His teacher, Niẓām al-Dīn Khāmūsh, gave him this advice: "If the effect of the irresistible power of God, Exalted is He, should manifest itself in you, beware of using that overwhelming force."

Sa'd al-Dīn Kāshgharī said:

> Some time after I had been given this advice, I experienced a state in which had I looked at someone he would immediately have lost consciousness; if he had come close to me he would have been completely destroyed. When this condition came upon me, I hid in a corner of my house and did not venture out of doors by night or by day for a whole fortnight. When I saw someone approaching from a distance, I would wave him away. This state eventually left me.

The following sayings of the venerable Kāshgharī are excerpted from a compilation made by one of his pupils:

> It is easier to reach God than to succeed in any worldly undertaking. To attain a worldly object, one must seek before one finds. But in the case of God, Exalted is He, the finding comes before the seeking, for without having found Him how could one be inclined to look for Him?

> To escape from heedlessness, God's people abstained completely from this world, abandoned everything and occupied themselves exclusively with the Exalted Truth.

If someone loved something, he would want the whole world to love it too.

It is God's custom not to allow access to the Truth before trials and tribulation have been experienced and pleasure and passions renounced.

My dear companions, know that God, in all His Majesty and Greatness, is very close to you. Be constantly aware that you are in His presence and always conduct yourselves, outwardly and inwardly, with propriety and respect.

To be united with God means not to exist.

Whoever is in one place is everywhere. Whoever is everywhere is nowhere.

Remember God constantly until you lose yourself.

Divine remembrance [dhikr] begins to bear fruit when it sheds its garb of letters and sounds in Arabic and Persian and is stripped bare of everything belonging to this world.

God, Exalted is He, taught the method of vigilant meditation to His own Messenger, on him be peace. Junaid al-Baghdādī said: "The Master who taught me vigilance was a cat watching a mouse-hole."

Mawlānā Jāmi's younger brother, Mawlānā Muḥammad, is reported to have said:

I used to work on alchemy and elixirs. In fact, I devoted much of my life to these pursuits. After prolonged experiments, I achieved certain promising results. Final success eluded me, however, so I vacillated between giving up and persevering with the work.

One day as I was walking in the market, I found myself in a crowd of people. Suddenly someone came up from behind and seized me by the neck. I looked round to see that it was the venerable Mawlānā

Sa'd al-Dīn. I begged him to tell me what was wrong and he said: "Brother:

Let me teach you an alchemy whose elixir has no price.
As a match for contentment, there's no alchemy can suffice."

Having recited this verse he immediately went his way. After this incident I lost all interest in alchemy and found perfect peace of mind. I realized that the venerable Mawlānā Sa'd al-Dīn had exerted his telekinetic powers out of pure compassion for this humble creature.

Many marvellous exploits of this kind are ascribed to him.

Mawlānā Kāshgharī died at the time of the noon prayer on Wednesday, 7 Jumādā-l'akhira 860/1456. His tomb is in Herāt.

He had two sons. The elder, Khwāja Muḥammad Akbar (better known as Khwāja Kilān), was a disciple of Khwāja Aḥrār. His younger son, Khwāja Muḥammad Aṣghar, was well versed in exoteric and esoteric learning. He died in 906/1500. Khwāja Muḥammad Kilān had two daughters, one of whom married the venerable Mawlānā Jāmī, while the other became the wife of Mawlānā Ḥusain Ṣafī, the author of the *Rashaḥāt.*

His most famous companions were Mawlānā 'Abd al-Raḥmān Jāmī, Shihāb al-Dīn Pirjandī, and 'Alā' al-Dīn Ābīzī.

The Exceptional Khwāja 'Ubaidallāh al-Aḥrār (Tashkandī)

One of the most exceptionally accomplished Sufis of the ninth/fifteenth century, Khwāja 'Ubaidallāh al-Aḥrār was born in Tashkent in the month of Ramaḍān 806/1404 and died at the age of eighty-nine* in the village of Kemāngirān near Samarqand. His tomb is in the outskirts of Samarqand.

His genealogy goes back to the Caliph 'Umar ibn al-Khaṭṭāb. He was initiated in the Sufi path by Mawlānā Ya'qūb Charkhī and met with many sages and mystics. He was still living when Mawlānā 'Abd al-Raḥmān Jāmī wrote about him in the *Rashaḥāt*:

> Today the connecting link in the noble chain of the Masters of Wisdom is the venerable Khwāja 'Ubaidallāh. It is our earnest hope and supplication that, by virtue of his noble being, this chain of transmission may continue unbroken till the Day of Resurrection.

♦ Khwāja Aḥrār's Family and Ancestors

The venerable Aḥrār belonged to a family associated with Tashkent. His father Khwāja Muḥammad Shāshī seems to have been a friend and follower of the Sufis. His grandfather was Khwāja Shihāb al-Dīn

*By the Islamic reckoning, the year of his death being 895/1490.

Shāshī, who is said to have been a wise and learned shaikh, endowed with spiritual states and charismatic powers. It was on account of his grandfather that some people later addressed Khwāja 'Ubaidallāh as "the Prince of Turkestan." Shaikh Shihāb al-Dīn particularly enjoyed the company of ecstatics. He engaged in commerce and agriculture. Of his two sons, one was 'Ubaidallāh Aḥrār's father, Khwāja Maḥmūd, while the other was his uncle, Khwāja Muḥammad.

When Khwāja Shihāb al-Dīn was near to death he asked to see his grandchildren. They brought him the children of his younger son, Khwāja Muḥammad, but he disapproved of them and reproached his son, saying: "I hardly expected such offspring from you." They then brought the infant 'Ubaidallāh into his presence, wrapped in a cloak. When Shihāb al-Dīn set eyes on the child,

> he became excited and said: "Sit me up!" When they had done so he took Khwāja 'Ubaidallāh in his arms, nuzzled all parts of his blessed body, and wept as he said: "This is the child I wanted. If only I could have lived to see him grow up! May this child soon bring honor to the world, currency to the sacred law and lustre to the Sufi path. May the kings of the world obey his orders and comply with his command and prohibition. May his achievements excel even those of the great shaikhs of the past."*

The venerable Shihāb al-Dīn went on to predict all that would happen to Khwāja 'Ubaidallāh throughout his life, then he again nuzzled his grandson before handing the child to his father, Khwāja Maḥmūd, and giving instructions that the boy should be well brought up.

One of Khwāja Aḥrār's ancestors was the celebrated Khwāja Muḥammad. This person was a native of Baghdād or, some say, of Khwārizm. He was a disciple of Imām Abū Bakr Shāshī, a great scholar of the Shāfi'ī school, and seems to have been a prominent figure in the society of Baghdād. His great-great-grandfather on his mother's side

---

**Rashaḥāt.*

was Shaikh 'Umar Bāghistānī, whose pedigree goes back by sixteen links to the Caliph 'Umar, by way of his son 'Abdallāh.

Shaikh 'Umar Bāghistānī was an eminent companion of Shaikh Ḥasan Bulghārī, who is described as an ecstatic saint. Shaikh Khāvand Ṭahūr was Shaikh 'Umar's son. He was proficient in exoteric and esoteric learning alike. After moving to Turkestan, he spent a long time with Tinguz Shaikh, a Yasavī Master.

According to the author of the *Rashaḥāt,* Shaikh Khāvand Ṭahūr produced works on Sufism in prose and verse. In one of his treatises he wrote: "Unification [*Tawḥīd*] can only mean separating the body from base desires for the sake of divine service, for God, Exalted is He, is One and it is absurd to unify the One." Khwāja Aḥrār would often cite the poems of Khāvand Ṭahūr in his own meetings and informal gatherings.

Khwāja Dāwūd was the son of Khāvand Ṭahūr and maternal grandfather of Khwāja 'Ubaidallāh. Shaikh 'Umar Bāgistānī's disciple, Bābā Ābrīz, and his sons, Shaikh Burhān al-Dīn Ābrīz and Shaikh Abū Sa'īd Ābrīz, are said to have been ecstatics. Another of Khwāja 'Ubaidallāh's ancestors was Mawlānā Tāj al-Dīn, one of the great men of his time according to the *Rashaḥāt.* His maternal uncle, Khwāja Ibrāhīm Shāshī, was a scholar of highly developed spirituality. In his youth he kept company with Sayyid Sharīf al-Jurjānī in Samarqand and studied exoteric science under him.

Khwāja 'Imād al-Mulk was his uncle by marriage. When 'Ubaidallāh Aḥrar was very small, he used to stay up late at night listening to the conversations between this uncle and his grandfather Shihāb al-Dīn Shāshī.

♦ His Childhood and Youth

By his own account, when Khwāja Aḥrār was one year old his family wanted to cut his hair. They were preparing the banquet customary on such occasions in Tashkent, when the news came that Tamerlane had died. Fear and panic spread among the people, who did not even pause to eat the food they had prepared, but emptied their cooking pots and took to the hills.

At that point in time the Khwāja's family was living in Bāghistān. According to the *Rashaḥāt*, a great enlightenment and intelligence showed on the child's forehead. Anyone who beheld the countenance of Khwāja Aḥrar, even at that tender age, would spontaneously bless him and praise him. It apparently never occurred to the Khwāja to be heedless of Allāh, and he supposed the same must apply to everyone else.

Again by his own account:

> I saw the Prophet Jesus in a dream. At that time I was just fifteen years old. The venerable Prophet was standing at the threshold of the tomb of Shaikh Abū Bakr Shāshī. I fell at his blessed feet. He raised my head from the ground, saying: "Do not be dismayed, for it is fitting that I should undertake your training." When I told this dream to certain others, they interpreted it to mean that I should become a physician. This explanation did not satisfy me, however, so I interpreted the dream in my own fashion. Since the venerable Jesus had been endowed with the power to bring the dead to life, I told myself that his willingness to train my unworthy self must be a sign that I would receive the ability to revive the hearts of men. This interpretation of mine was shortly to be verified.

In another of his dreams he saw the noble Messenger, who commanded him to carry him on his shoulders to the summit of a mountain. The venerable Prophet then said: "I already knew that you possessed the strength to do this. My only purpose was to demonstrate the fact." In yet another dream he witnessed an example of the supernatural power of the venerable Khwāja Naqshband.

His own story continues: "Early in my development, I experienced such inner humility that I would fall at the feet of everyone I happened to meet, making no distinction between freeman and slave, white and black, young and old, master and servant. I would humbly implore them for spiritual aid."*

"They say that the followers of Khwāja 'Abd al-Khāliq heard nothing but the remembrance of God, even in the midst of crowds. I experienced this myself when I was only eighteen."

In his youth the venerable Khwāja Aḥrār seems to have been quite poor. He says that when he was in Herāt at the time of Mīrzā Shāhrukh, he "didn't have a bean." He goes on to say:

> The turban on my head was in tatters and I could only afford one kaftan a year, which wore so thin that the cotton padding showed through. I worked in the service of many different people but never had a horse or donkey of my own. My clothes were so thin and so short that the lower part of my body never got warm in winter. In all the time I spent away from home in search of God, I cannot remember once having a couple of ewers of warm water for my ablutions, even in the depth of winter. When I needed to restore my ritual purity, I would sometimes leave the company of Shaikh Bahā' al-Dīn 'Umar and go into the town for my ablutions. I would sometimes think: "If only the venerable Shaikh would consider letting his dervishes have a drop of warm water, so they could do their ablutions here in the icy winter." But this was never granted.

During the five years he stayed in Herāt, he would accept nothing from anyone for all his poverty and need. According to the *Rashaḥāt,* he never accepted any kind of present as long as he lived.

Regarding his poverty, he tells us himself how he went one day to visit Sayyid Qāsim Tabrīzī. The Sayyid gave him a bowl of food, half of which he had eaten, and said: "Hey, Prince of Turkestan, as these hardships have been our screen, may worldly wealth become your screen before long." Khwāja Aḥrār says: "When the venerable Sayyid spoke these words, I was extremely poor, with not a worldly thing to call my own. I acknowledge that I owe my present wealth and

---

**Rashaḥāt.*

affluence to this blessing breathed by the venerable Qāsim Tabrīzī."

When he reached the age of twenty-two, his maternal uncle Khwāja Ibrāhīm brought him from Tashkent to be educated in Samarqand. His interest in esoteric wisdom and Sufism was so passionate, however, that he could make no headway in ordinary learning. His uncle tried to make him persevere, but he spent all his time attending the meetings of the Sufis of Samarqand and listening to their conversations. He tried to pursue his formal studies, but only succeeded in making himself ill. His efforts resulted in serious eyestrain, and he was eventually compelled to abandon them altogether. In later life, he would say jokingly: "My education got as far as page two of the elementary reader."

After spending two years like this in Samarqand, at the age of twenty-four he moved to Herāt. There he stayed for five years, mostly in the company of Sufi Masters. He returned to his native Tashkent at the age of twenty-nine.

It was at this stage of his life that he became interested in agriculture. He was blessed with remarkable success in a farming venture started with one partner and a pair of oxen. In a short space of time he had become a rich landowner, with a huge income from his crops, livestock, and rents. In this connection he used to say: "My property has been so blessed by God, Exalted is He, that my tithe to the court granary of Sultan Aḥmad Mīrzā amounts to eighty million measures of grain per annum." When asked why he should have received such bounty, he replied: "My wealth is for the benefit of the poor, that is why."

According to the *Rashaḥāt*:

> The venerable Khwāja one day explained the meaning of the noble Qur'ānic Verse: "Surely We have given you abundance." He said that the Masters of Wisdom interpret it to mean: "We have given you the vision of Oneness in multiplicity." He then went on to say: "For those who achieve this degree of insight, every atom in the universe will surely become a mirror, in which they will behold the everlasting beauty of the Divine Countenance."

♦ His Spiritual Journey and the People He Met

As a young man on the spiritual path, the venerable Khwāja 'Ubaidallāh was devoted to the service of ordinary people. In the very early hours he would go to the great public baths in Herāt and work as an unpaid attendant. "Sometimes," he tells us, "I would attend to five or six cubicles at a time. To avoid taking payment, I used to leave as soon as my work was done. When they looked for me, I was nowhere to be found."

He used to say: "It was not in books that I discovered Sufism, but through serving ordinary folk. Everyone has a road to follow and mine has been the road of service. That is why service is what I love and value most of all. If I have high hopes of someone, I always recommend the way of service to him."

From his close associates and those who served with him for many years, we know that Khwāja Aḥrār was the very embodiment of refined behavior, both inwardly and outwardly, "in public and in private." Abū Sa'īd Awbahī, his dervish for thirty-five years, has this to say about him: "In all those years I spent in his service, I never saw him spit out the skin of a grape, apple, pear, or quince, whether he was alone or in company. By night or by day I never saw him sitting in any but a kneeling posture, even when he was on his own. To my knowledge, he never once behaved unpleasantly or showed a disagreeable mood."

He was always extremely friendly and attentive to those around him, taking great pains to ensure the ease and comfort of his companions and loved ones.

The venerable Aḥrār met and associated with many of Khwāja Naqshband's chief disciples and their deputies. Before coming to Khurāsān, he was close to Shaikh Ṣadr al-Dīn Yamanī, the follower of Shaikh Awḥad al-Dīn Kirmānī. In Samarqand he met with Sayyid Qāsim Tabrīzī, a poet and sage endowed with the spirit of Reality and Liberation in a high degree. After moving to Khurāsān, he was to spend much time at Herāt in the company of this remarkable person and other prominent shaikhs of that city.

When he moved from Tashkent to Samarqand, at the age of twenty-two, he became a regular attender at the meetings of Mawlānā Sa'd al-Dīn Kāshgharī. He would also go and sit in silence at the feet of Mawlānā Niẓām al-Dīn Khāmūsh. The *Nafaḥāt* records his own account of an incident that occurred at this time:

> At the age of twenty-two I went to Samarqand with the intention of pursuing an ordinary course of study. At that time Mawlānā Niẓām al-Dīn Khāmūsh was a professor at the Academy of Ulugh Bey. I had already heard about this person's ecstatic and contemplative faculties. When I arrived at the Academy he was giving a lecture, so I sat in a corner and listened in silence. When the lecture was over, he asked me: "What is the reason for your silence?" He then proceeded to answer his own question, saying: "There are two kinds of silence. The first comes about because the person who is silent has left the world of ordinary humanity. This kind of silence is sacred to its owner. The other kind is the silence one keeps while still in the ordinary human condition; this is a dangerous snare."

In Bukhārā he met with Mawlānā Ḥamīd al-Dīn Shāshi and sat in the company of Khwāja 'Alā' al-Dīn Ghujdawānī. Passing by way of Merv en route from Bukhārā to Khurāsān, he came to Herāt and stayed there for four years. During this period he frequented the meetings of Sayyid Qāsim Tabrīzī and Shaikh Bahā' al-Dīn 'Umar. He is also said to have visited Shaikh Zain al-Dīn Khwāfī at this time.

Later, in Balkh, he associated with Mawlānā Ḥusām al-Dīn Parsā al-Balkhī, one of the deputies of Khwāja 'Alā' al-Dīn 'Aṭṭār. After visiting the tomb of 'Alā' al-Dīn 'Aṭṭār in Chigāniyān, he went to Khuluftu and there paid allegiance to Mawlānā Ya'qūb Charkhī. He stayed with his teacher for three months before returning to Herāt, where he spent a further five years before going back to his native Tashkent and involving himself in agriculture.

"Until my twenty-ninth year," he tells us, "I wandered in foreign parts, returning to Tashkent five years before the plague year." As the plague occurred in the year 840/1436, he must have gone home in the year 835.

♦ Experiences with Sayyid Qāsim Tabrīzī

Khwāja Aḥrār speaks with great respect of Sayyid Qāsim Tabrīzī, as the most important of all the sages with whom he had contact: "In all my life," he tells us, "I never met a more highly developed person. I enjoyed the company of other great shaikhs of the age, but I was always moved to leave them in the end. But the well being I experienced in the presence of the venerable Sayyid Qāsim seemed never to diminish. Whenever I entered his presence, I used to see the whole universe revolve around him, becoming non-existent and unmanifest in his being."

'Ubaidallāh Aḥrār was a great favorite of Sayyid Qāsim Tabrīzī. He normally entertained his visitors only briefly, but never encouraged Khwāja Aḥrār to leave. Contrary to his usual practice, he instructed his people to admit the Khwāja whenever he arrived.

At their first meeting, he asked the Khwāja's name. When he learned that it was 'Ubaidallāh, he said: "You must attain the reality of your name."* As the *Rashaḥāt* explains:

> The venerable Sayyid was indicating by these words that to deserve a name meaning "Servant of God" a person ought to know Him . . . The name of the Divine Essence is comprehensive and embraces all the attributes, so that he who knows the significance of the name of the Essence will also come to understand all the other names . . . To bear the name "Servant of God" is therefore the privilege of a most highly perfected saint, in whom the contemplation of the Essential Illumination has been realized. The "contemplation of the Essential Illumination" is that beyond which no veil or curtain remains. Only when this is achieved does transformation become permanent. The principal holder of this station is the chief of the

*The name 'Ubaidallāh is a variant of 'Abdallāh, meaning "Servant of God."

Prophets, Muḥammad Muṣṭafā, Allāh bless him and give him peace. In every age it is deputed to one perfect individual known as the Cardinal of cardinals [*Quṭb al-aqṭāb*]. When the venerable Sayyid said: "You must achieve the realization of your own name," he meant: "You now bear the outer form of the name Servant-of-God. May you deserve it in reality also and become the supreme Cardinal and great Caliph of your age."

One of Sayyid Qāsim's associates, Mawlānā Fatḥallāh of Tabrīz, reports that whenever Khwāja Aḥrār visited the venerable Sayyid and sat in his presence, Qāsim Tabrīzī would start speaking spontaneously of the most profound secrets of the Divine Reality. Wondrous truths and subtleties would emerge in the course of the conversation. This never happened at other times.

One day, when Khwāja 'Ubaidallāh had left after such a conversation, Sayyid Qāsim said to Fatḥallāh:

> Sufi sayings are indeed most enjoyable, but it is not enough merely to tell and hear them. If you wish to attain the felicity which is the goal of all earnest seekers, you should hold tight to the robe of that young Turkestani and never let it go, for he is destined to become the wonder of the age, the jewel of our time. Many noble works will be accomplished through him. May the world soon be illumined by the light of his sainthood, so that dead hearts may be revived to eternal life by the blessed elixir of his company and be crowned with the spirit of love and affection.

One day Sayyid Qāsim said to Khwāja 'Ubaidallāh:

> Do you know why wisdom and truth are so little in evidence these days? It is because the essential foundation of inner purification is lacking. Purification is impossible without lawful nourishment. Since this is hard to come by nowadays, there is also a dearth of that inner purity which is the source of divine secrets. As long as I could, I

> made a living by sewing skull-caps, but my hand became paralyzed and I had to give up this work. I then sold the library I had inherited and used the capital to get into business. I now make a living from trade.

In his youth the venerable Sayyid spent much of his time in the company of ecstatics. He tells us:

> When I was in Anatolia, I made enquiries about ecstatics and dervishes crazy with divine love. They told me where I could find a certain person answering this description. I went to look for him and whom should I find but Mawlānā Jānī, who had been my fellow student in Tabrīz. Speaking in Eastern Turkish, I asked: "Mawlānā Jānī, do you recognize me?" "You are Mawlānā Sayyid," said he. I then asked what had happened to him and he said: "Like you, I was all confused. Something was always pulling me this way or that. Then, suddenly, something appeared and took me out of myself." He then switched to Anatolian Turkish as he added: "I found peace, I found peace . . ."

According to Khwāja Aḥrār, tears would stream from Sayyid Qāsim's eyes whenever he told this story.

Khwāja Aḥrār was attracted by the experiences of Shaikh Bahā' al-Dīn 'Umar, his contemporary among the Sufis of Khurāsān. This person was disinclined to entertain visitors and from time to time, in accordance with the practice of his Order, he would go into retreat. Nevertheless, Khwāja 'Ubaidallāh used to visit him two or three times a week during the five years he spent in Herāt. He tells us:

> On one of these visits of mine he asked me as usual for news of the city.
>
> "There are two kinds of news," said I.
>
> "What are they?" he asked.

I replied: "Shaikh Zain al-Dīn Khwāfī and his followers say that everything is *from* God,* while Sayyid Qāsim Tabrīzī and his associates say that everything *is* God.† What do you say?"

"Shaikh Zain al-Dīn's men are right," he said, and he went on to adduce evidence in support of their assertion. As I listened, however, I realized that his arguments actually confirmed the view of Sayyid Qāsim's party. When I pointed this out, Shaikh Bahā' produced further arguments tending to support the view of Sayyid Qāsim. I then understood his intention: he was hinting that while it was necessary to display superficial agreement with Zain al-Dīn Khwāfi's position, he secretly shared the view of Sayyid Qāsim.

♦ Meeting His Spiritual Director, Mawlānā Ya'qūb Charkhī

The venerable Khwāja Aḥrar gives the following account of his meeting with his spiritual director, Mawlānā Ya'qūb Charkhī:

> After four years in Herāt, I set out for Khuluftu with the intention of seeking instruction from Mawlānā Ya'qūb Charkhī. I had heard him highly recommended some years earlier by a man of great refinement, a merchant of Chil-Dukhtarān.
>
> When I reached the province of Chigāniyān, where Mawlānā Ya'qūb was living, I fell ill and had to break my journey for twenty days. During that time I heard so many negative things about Mawlānā Charkhī that I almost gave up the idea of seeking him out. I had traveled a great distance, however, so it did not seem sensible to turn back without meeting him.
>
> When I entered his presence he treated me with the utmost courtesy and kindness. But when I returned to see him the next day he appeared extremely angry and his manner toward me was quite harsh and rude. I put this down to the hesitancy I was feeling as a result of the rumors I had heard about him. After a while he reverted to being

*In Persian, *hame az ust* (all is from Him).

†In Persian, *hame ūst* (all is He).

infinitely kind and attentive. He told me how he had come to meet Khwāja Bahā' al-Dīn Naqshband, then stretched out his hand and said, "Come here and give me your oath of allegiance."

At that moment I saw in his face a repulsive whiteness like leprosy and I felt no inclination to take his hand in allegiance. The venerable Mawlānā understood my feeling of repugnance and immediately withdrew his hand. As if changing his clothes, he suddenly transformed his appearance and assumed such a beautiful countenance that my reservations vanished and I found myself spontaneously embracing him.

Ya'qūb Charkhī again held out his hand as he said: "The venerable Khwāja Bahā' al-Dīn Naqshband took my hand in his and said: 'Your hand is my hand, whoever holds your hand has held my hand.' This hand is the hand of Khwāja Bahā' al-Dīn, so take hold of it." I immediately took his blessed hand in mine and he instructed me in the method of negation and affirmation through numerical awareness.*

Mawlānā Charkhī added: "This is what I received from the venerable Khwāja Naqshband. If you prefer, you may train your own pupils by way of ecstasy."

After three months in his company, Mawlānā Ya'qūb gave me permission to leave. On the day of parting, he gave me a complete explanation and clarification of the Way of the Masters. He described the method of bonding heart to heart and said: "Go gently in teaching this path. May you guide capable seekers to their destination."

♦ Some Sayings of Khwāja Aḥrār

[In explanation of the Qur'ānic verse: "All praise belongs to Allāh, Lord of All the Worlds."†] Praise has its inception and its consummation. Praise reaches its consummation when the servant realizes

*Translator's note: see page 33.

†*Al-ḥamdu lillāhi rabbi-l'ālamīn* (1:2).

that he is but the point of manifestation where God, Exalted is He, praises Himself; when he recognizes his own non-existence and when he sees that neither Essence nor attributes nor actions belong to him at all.

[Concerning the Qur'ānic verse: "And be with the faithful and true."*]

With loving friends rejoice;
Love should ever be your choice.
From those who are not loving, flee,
High and mighty though they be.

[On the Qur'ānic verse: "Say 'Allāh!' then leave them."†] This means: "Leave the attributes and return to the Essence."

[On the Qur'ānic verse: "It is the same to them whether you warn them . . ."‡] This probably refers to those who are immersed in the wonder of Love. Lost in ecstatic contemplation of the Essence, they are unaware of the existence of anything but God.

[Concerning the Prophetic saying: "To me, together with Allāh."§] The mysterious reality of the venerable Messenger is so closely and everlastingly attached to the Exalted Truth that nothing else could intervene between them.

There are two kinds of pride. The first is the common variety, which is unacceptable. Admissible pride is total dedication to the Exalted Truth. This genuine pride is conducive to annihilation.

Khwāja Muḥammad Parsā says that constant divine remembrance reaches a stage where the remembrance and the heart become one single reality. In my opinion, this must mean that the reality of dhikr is something transcending words and sounds, while the reality of the

---

**Wa-kūnū ma'a-lṣādiqīn* (9: 119).
†*Quli-llāhu thumma dharhum* (6: 91).
‡*Sawā'un 'alaihim a-andhartahum* (2: 6).
§*Lī ma'a-llāh.*

heart is a subtle awareness transcending the categories of quality and quantity. When constant remembrance reaches perfection, these two realities unite and it becomes impossible to distinguish one from the other. At that moment nothing can penetrate the heart except the object of remembrance (God) and both remembrance and heart become annihilated in Him.

Niẓām al-Dīn Khāmūsh once asked me: "Is silence to be preferred or is it better to speak?" Before I could answer, he went on to say: "If you have been liberated from your own existence, nothing you do can become an obstacle; but if you are trapped within the confines of your being, then whatever you do is harmful."*

Shaikh Abū-l Qāsim Jurjānī said: "Seek the company of someone in whose being you merge completely, or who merges completely in yours, or together with whom you become extinguished in the Exalted Truth so that neither of you remains."

In order to achieve non-being, the traveller must carry self-abasement and humiliation to such lengths that he comes to witness the Divine Beauty in the mirror of annihilation and non-existence.

Nothing is so effective as misfortune and tribulation for purifying one's inner being. Pain and suffering rend the coarsest human veils. Such is my own belief, though it is not shared by any friend or companion.

The universal aim is this: that one's subtle awareness should be directed permanently toward the Exalted Truth.

Such a close contact with reality must be attained that neither water can wash it away nor fire burn it up.

According to the author of the *Rashaḥāt,* 'Ubaidallāh Aḥrār once

---

*Compare the famous stanza of the venerable Abū Sa'īd Abū-l Khair:

With You, my every pretence is prayer,
Without You, all my prayers are pretence.

said to him in private: "The sum of all the various sciences is the explanation of the Qur'an, the Prophetic Tradition, and Islamic jurisprudence. The sum of all these is the science of Sufism. The sum and subject matter of Sufism is the question of Being. They say that at all levels there is but one single Being, which becomes apparent through its own ideation. This is a very difficult and subtle topic. To reflect upon it, both reason and imagination must be brought into play. Starting with a keen intelligence, one must devote one's entire effort to polishing the mirror of one's own reality until no trace of the world remains. As this mirror is purified of unreality, one's subtle awareness begins to reflect the light of Being and the Reality of Being shows its true face."

The Birds gathered together and set off to visit Sīmurg (the King of Birds). One by one they made their excuses and turned back. None reached Sīmurg but those who had something of Sīmurg within them.

Absolute annihilation does not mean becoming unconscious of oneself. Annihilation means the real experience of detaching oneself from attributes and actions and confirming that God is the real doer. This explains the Sufi riddle: "There is no struggle of denial and affirmation."

Is our ultimate goal presence and direct contemplation? Or is it annihilation and non-being? Some great sages would seem to maintain the former view, but in reality the goal is annihilation and non-being. To be subject to presence and contemplation is to be subject to something "other."

Divine contemplation has two meanings: one is to witness the singularity of the Sacred Essence through the veil of manifestations; this is what the Sufis call the vision of Oneness in multiplicity. The other is to behold the Pure Essence in total abstraction.

The ultimate goal of Sufism is the degree attained by the perfect saints. Direct contemplation is not lost at this stage, unless through complete absorption in the vision of Reality.

> To know the secret of destiny is to be at peace. For it is to be aware that the apparent universe is entirely non-existent and that God is the Reality behind all manifest forms. The peace such knowledge brings is like that of the waves returning to the ocean.
>
> Scholars like Abū Ḥanīfa and al-Shāfi'ī discussed the external aspect of the sacred law. Of the reality of Love they had no knowledge.

♦ Some Marvelous Exploits of Khwāja Aḥrār

As recorded in the *Rashaḥāt* and *Nafaḥāt,* in his youth, he was strolling one day with Mawlānā Sa'd al-Dīn Kāshgharī. They stopped to watch a wrestling match in the Herāt bazaar. A well-built champion was getting the better of a weaker fellow. Sa'd al-Dīn and Khwāja Aḥrār decided to test the development of their spiritual powers by lending moral support to the weaker wrestler:

> No sooner had we begun to concentrate on the underdog than a remarkable change came over him. He caught his bulky opponent in a hold and lifted him off the floor. Then he turned him upside-down and landed him flat on his back. Cheers erupted from the astonished crowd, to whom the cause of this dramatic upset remained a mystery.
>
> I noticed that Mawlānā Sa'd al-Dīn still had his eyes half shut. I tugged at his sleeve and said: "That's enough. Don't concentrate any longer."

A friend of his relates:

> I was with Khwāja Aḥrār in Firkat. One day he asked for an ink-holder and pen. He wrote the name Abū Sa'īd Mīrzā on a piece of paper, which he then folded and put inside his turban. At that time, the name and title of Sultan Abū Sa'īd Mīrzā were still unheard of. Some of the Khwāja's relatives were curious to know whose name he had written down and then placed so respectfully on his head.

He explained: "This name belongs to a man whose subjects we may all become, for he is destined to rule Tashkent, Samarqand, and Khurāsān."

A few days later the fame of Sultan Abū Sa'id Mīrzā spread from Turkestan. It seems the Sultan had a dream in which, at a sign from Khwāja Aḥmad Yasavī, Khwāja Aḥrār recited to him the first Sūra of the Qur'ān. In his dream, he asked Khwāja Yasavī the name of the venerable Aḥrār, whose features he retained in his memory after awaking from sleep. He also recalled the name he had been given, so he enquired among his entourage to see if anyone knew the person to whom it belonged. On learning that such a person was to be found in Tashkent, Mīrzā took horse at once and set off in that direction.

He found Khwāja 'Ubaidallāh waiting to meet him in Firkat and he fell at his feet, saying: "By God, this is the holy man I saw in my dream!" He humbly implored his blessing, which was granted.

The venerable Aḥrār won Mīrzā's heart completely, treating him with great kindness and attention. He was also a great help and inspiration to him later on, during his political career.

When Sultan Maḥmūd Mīrzā proposed to seize Samarqand from his brother, Sultan Aḥmad Mīrzā, Khwāja Aḥrār tried to dissuade him. He pointed out that Samarqand enjoyed the protection of the saints and warned him that to draw the sword against his brother would be immoral and contrary to the sacred law of Islam. But Sultan Maḥmūd would hear none of this. He marched on Samarqand. When the armies met in battle, Khwāja 'Ubaidallāh and three of his companions exerted their supernatural powers. A violent rainstorm ensued. The army of Maḥmūd Mīrzā was thrown into confusion, his commanders took fright, and the siege of Samarqand was lifted.

Khwāja Aḥrār had his opponents, for there were those who could not conceive the idea that a spiritual teacher might also be a rich trader and landowner. He was nevertheless renowned for the charismatic powers he demonstrated to friends and opponents alike, especially to the rulers of that period.

He used to say: "Had I assumed the role of shaikh, none of my contemporaries would have found any pupils. But our business is to protect the Muslims from the evils of tyranny. It is therefore our duty to make contact with kings, winning their hearts through friendly intercourse."

He also said: "Such power has been conferred on me by the pure grace of God, Exalted is He, that—if I wished—I could write a letter to the Emperor of China, who claims divinity, and charm him into forsaking his throne and running barefoot to my door. Nevertheless, I humbly await God's bidding."

♦ His Death

Khwāja Aḥrār fell sick in the month of Muḥarram, 895/1489. His final illness lasted eighty-nine days, and he was eighty-nine years old when he died, on a Friday night at the end of the month of Rabī'u-l'awwal, 895/1490.

Mawlānā Abū Sa'īd Awbahī attended the venerable Khwāja during his final sickness. He relates how on Wednesday, 20 Rabī'u-l'awwal 895, the Khwāja ignored his poor health and set out for the village of Kemāngirān. His condition was worse on the Thursday, but he managed to travel all day, reaching Kemāngirān in time for the late evening prayer. There he stayed for seven days. On the seventh day, Friday, his strength began to ebb. On the last day of the month, he performed his sunset prayer by nods and signs. A few hours later, the venerable Khwāja Nāṣir al-Dīn 'Ubaidallāh al-Aḥrar had breathed his last.

During his illness, the Khwāja was very careful not to fall behind with his prayers. When he was in the throes of death, an earthquake occurred in Samarqand. This was felt by people gathered in the mosque for midday prayers. To those who knew of the Khwāja's condition, it seemed to be an omen of his death. As soon as the congregational prayer was over, they set off on the walk to Kemāngirān. At the very moment of his death a second and more violent earthquake occurred in Samarqand.

Sultan Ahmad Mīrzā arrived with his retinue in time to be near the Khwāja during his last moments. They conveyed his body to Samarqand in a funeral procession. After the ritual washing and enshrouding, the funeral prayers were performed. The congregation included the nobles and notables of Samarqand, as well as a throng of ordinary folk.

His children and grandchildren constructed a fine mausoleum over his grave, which became a place of visitation.

♦ Khwāja Aḥrār's Descendants and Companions

♦ Khwāja Muḥammad ibn 'Abdallāh

Khwāja Aḥrār's elder son, born by his first wife, was Muḥammad ibn 'Abdallāh, better known as "Khwājagān." Well versed in all branches of learning, he seems to have possessed insight and special powers like those of his father. We are told that Khwāja 'Ubaidallāh treated his son with respect and formal politeness. When the Uzbeks conquered Samarqand he found a refuge near Andijān, where he died and lies buried.

He was the son-in-law of Sayyid Taqī al-Dīn Muḥammad Kirmānī, whose daughter bore him three sons and two daughters. When this wife died he married a daughter of Khwāja Muḥammad Niẓām. This second wife also bore him three sons and two daughters.

According to the *Nafaḥāt,* the venerable Khwājagān had the following sons, in order of age: Khwāja 'Abd al-Hādī, Khwāja Khāvand Maḥmūd, Khwāja 'Abd al-Ḥaqq, Khwāja 'Abd al-'Alīm, Khwāja Muḥammad Yūsuf, Khwāja 'Abd al-Shahīd, Khwāja 'Abd al-Fayḍ. All of them were Masters of Wisdom.

♦ Khwāja 'Abd al-Ḥaqq

Of the venerable 'Ubaidallāh's grandchildren, the most notable is Khwāja 'Abd al-Ḥaqq, the third of Muḥammmad ibn 'Abdallāh's eight sons.* Khwāja Aḥrār taught him how to do dhikr when he was only twelve years old, describing the boy as a future Master.

The light of sainthood and signs of charisma appeared in Khwāja 'Abd al-Ḥaqq after his grandfather's death. Thirty years later, in the year 925 of the Hijra, he succeeded to Khwāja Aḥrar's teaching rug.

---

*Editor's note: The section above indicates six or seven sons. This text reflects the original.

Khwāja 'Ubaidallāh al-Aḥrār

- Khwāja Muḥammad ibn 'Abdallāh (son)
- Khwāja 'Abd al-Ḥaqq (grandson)
- Khwāja Muḥammad Yaḥyā (son)
- Mawlānā Sayyid Ḥasan
- Mawlānā Sirāj al-Dīn Qāsim
- Mīr 'Abd al-Awwal
- Mawlānā Ja'far
- Mawlānā Burhān al-Dīn Khuttalānī
- Mawlānā Luṭfallāh Khuttalānī
- Mawlānā Shaikh Idāmallāh
- Mawlānā Sulṭān Aḥmad
- Mawlānā Abū Sa'īd Awbahī
- Mawlānā Muḥammad Qāḍī
- Mawlānā Khwāja 'Alī Tashkandī
- Shaikh Ḥabīb Najjār Tashkandī
- Mawlānā Nūr al-Dīn Tashkandī
- Mawlānā Zāda Otrārī
- Mawlānā Nāṣir al-Dīn Otrārī
- Hindū Khwāja Turkistānī
- Mawlānā Ismā'īl Firhatī
- Shaikh Faḍlī Ilāhī
- Sayyid Aḥmad al-Bukhārī

Figure 8

♦ Khwāja Muḥammad Yaḥyā

Khwāja Muḥammad Yaḥyā was the younger son of the venerable 'Ubaidallāh Aḥrār, by his second wife. He was a great favorite with his father. Toward the end of his life, Khwāja Aḥrār made him his lieutenant and appointed him keeper of his tomb.

Whenever Khwāja Yaḥyā came to his father's meetings, Khwāja Aḥrār would speak of the most profound truths, addressing his words to his son. The venerable 'Abd al-Raḥmān Jāmī was a great believer in Khwāja Muḥammad Yaḥyā. He said: "Knowledge is the dominant characteristic in the venerable Khwājagān, while Khwāja Yaḥyā is more inclined to ecstasy."

After his father's death, he made it a custom to kneel in vigil by his tomb from just after late evening prayers until dawn. Khwāja Aḥrar's companions were thrilled to find him taking after his father in friendliness and insight. He also had psychic powers like those of his father, but he seldom displayed them.

Khwāja Muḥammad Yaḥyā had all his goods and property confiscated in the year 906/1500-1, when Samarqand was seized by the Uzbek chieftain Shāh Bakht Khān. He was on the road to Khurāsān when he and his two sons, Khwāja Zakariyā and Khwāja Muḥammad Bāqī, were attacked and martyred by an Uzbek detachment three hundred strong. He had received a spiritual indication of the fate that awaited him. His body was interred beside his father's tomb.

Note: The *Thamarāt al-Fu'ād* mentions another son of 'Ubaidallāh al-Aḥrār, named Khwāja Muḥammad Amīn.

♦ Mawlānā Sayyid Ḥasan

Mawlānā Sayyid Ḥasan was a great friend of Khwāja Aḥrār. His father took him into the Khwāja's presence one day when he was just a little boy. The Khwāja happened to have a dish of honey in front of him, and the child immediately sat down and started eating it. When Khwāja Aḥrār asked his name, he said: "Honey." 'Ubaidallāh laughingly praised the child's capacity for total immersion in the thing he loved. Taking the boy from his father, he taught him to read and also gave him spiritual training. In later years he held Sayyid Ḥasan in very high esteem.

♦ Mawlānā Sirāj al-Dīn Qāsim

Mawlānā Sirāj al-Dīn Qāsim was a disciple and servant of the venerable Aḥrār, to whom he stuck so close that they nicknamed him "the Khwāja's shadow." In the early days he used to prune the Khwāja's fruit trees. His strongest disposition was toward ecstasy and non-being. Mawlānā Jāmī seems to have considered him superior to all the rest of 'Ubaidallāh Aḥrār's disciples. We are told that the Khwāja once fell seriously ill and Mawlānā Qāsim wished to sacrifice himself to save his teacher. Over the protests of the venerable Aḥrar, he took the disease upon himself and died of it, while the Khwāja recovered.

His death occurred in the year 891. As he was dying, he fixed his gaze on the countenance of the venerable Khwāja, who wept as he said: "He had no equal in annihilation and inner abstraction; who is left to us now?"

♦ Mīr 'Abd al-Awwal

The son-in-law of Khwāja Aḥrār, Mīr 'Abd al-Awwal was a native of Nīshāpūr. Khwāja Aḥrār trained him through abasement and humiliation. Having entered the service of 'Ubaidallāh in Transoxiana, he devoted seven years to self-discipline and spiritual exercises. In all that time, his teacher ignored him completely; if he happened to catch his eye, he would turn him out of the meeting and subject him to harsh treatment. But at the end of the seven years he gave his daughter to Mīr 'Abd al-Awwal in marriage, making him his son-in-law.

He tells us how the Khwāja reduced him to "scorched earth." When he looked at himself, he "seemed as useless as a rotten tooth."

These words reminded the author of the *Rashaḥāt* that the Khwāja once said:

> God, Exalted is He, appears to treat his saints harshly in this world, but there is grace concealed within that harshness. Through that hidden

> grace, God uses His apparent harshness to cleanse the inner reality of His servants till they are liberated from the ordinary human condition. The reverse applies to those God does not love, for He uses apparent grace to bind their inner being more tightly to the coarse physical world, while His secret harshness deprives them of the world of liberation and its spiritual delights.

Mīr 'Abd al-Awwal died in the year 905/1500, forty days before the martyrdom of Khwāja Muḥammad Yaḥyā and his two sons.

♦ Mawlānā Ja'far

Mawlānā Ja'far was a scholar who was both practical and wise. This companion of Khwāja Aḥrār had a strong disposition toward ecstasy and non-being. During his ritual prayers, he would recite long passages from the Qur'ān. He could hardly raise his head from prostration because of the intense rapture he experienced during worship. He spoke but little.

He is reported as saying:

> My heart soon grew weary of formal studies and I yearned to follow the people of God. One night I dreamt that I had entered the Khwāja's service. I asked him: "When does the servant reach God?" He replied: "Only when he disappears from himself." This dream affected me so deeply that I left college straight away and went to Aḥrār. "Mawlānā Ja'far," said he, "do you know when the servant may reach the Lord? Only when he loses himself in the service of God."

He died in 893/1488. All the associates of Khwāja Aḥrār were present at his funeral. Three days later they held a feast in honor of his soul, slaughtering eighty sheep for the roast dish alone.

♦ Mawlānā Burhān al-Dīn Khuttalānī

Mawlānā Burhān al-Dīn Khuttalānī was one of Khwāja Aḥrār's chief companions and an eminent scholar. He completed his exoteric studies at an early age. For about forty years, he was inseparable from the company of Khwāja 'Ubaidallāh. He tells the story of how, at the request of Sultan Aḥmad Mīrzā, Khwāja Aḥrār took him and some other companions on an expedition into Turkestan one very severe winter. He describes the hardships of the journey to the village of Shāhrukhiyya, where the Khwāja so charmed the Mongols and Uzbeks who came there to plunder, that they spontaneously discarded their idols and embraced the faith of Islam, having first handed over to the Khwāja some two thousand prisoners they had captured.

Khwāja 'Ubaidallāh sent the captives back to their homelands. As for the invaders, he appointed experts to teach them the Qur'ān and the doctrines of Islam.

Mawlānā Khuttalānī died eight days before Mawlānā Ja'far. Both of them had received medical treatment at the hands of a doctor from Khurāsān. This doctor found the venerable Khwāja 'Ubaidallāh in a very angry mood: "He addressed me with harsh words, saying: 'You have killed two of my men, a third like whom is not to be found on the face of this earth. Even if the seven levels of earth and the seven layers of heaven were filled with pure gold, their value would not be matched.'"*

♦ Mawlānā Luṭfallāh Khuttalānī

Mawlānā Luṭfallāh Khuttalānī was the nephew of Mawlānā Burhān al-Dīn and a favorite of Khwāja Aḥrār. He was well versed in sacred law and mysticism. We find him described as a cheerful and humorous person, whose wit amused Khwāja 'Ubaidallāh.

One night in a dream he saw the blessed Prophet, who appeared exceptionally beautiful. In a meeting the next day, the venerable Khwāja looked at him as he said: "People dream of the venerable Messenger in various forms." At this, the Mawlānā tells us: "I saw in the Khwāja the very same beauty I had seen in the Messenger of Allāh, on him be peace. As a result of this vision I became quite addicted to Khwāja Aḥrār."

**Rashaḥāt.*

♦ Mawlānā Shaikh Idāmallāh

Mawlānā Shaikh Idāmallāh was a companion of Khwāja 'Ubaidallāh and his steward for many years. While in the Khwāja's service, he observed constant austerity and self-discipline.

♦ Mawlānā Sulṭān Aḥmad

Mawlānā Sulṭān Aḥmad was a religious scholar, well versed in both exoteric and esoteric learning. He took leave from Khwāja 'Ubaidallāh to go on Pilgrimage, reentering his service after his return from Mecca.

♦ Mawlānā Abū Sa'īd Awbahī

Mawlānā Abū Sa'īd Awbahī* was a close companion of Khwāja Aḥrār, in whose service he spent thirty years. He had been a student at the Academy of Ulugh Bey but abandoned his studies when Sufism became his passionate interest. Leaving the college in Samarqand, he set out for Kūh-i Nūr ("Mountain of Light") to join Shaikh Ilyās 'Ishqī, of whom he had heard good reports. He tells us:

> By coincidence, my road passed by the door of Khwāja Aḥrār's school. I saw him ride up from somewhere and dismount from his horse by the gate. It struck me that I had never seen the Khwāja before, so I decided to postpone my visit to Kūh-i Nūr until I had made his acquaintance. I followed him into the school, where I saw him sitting with a group of disciples in the hall. I went in and sat facing him. For a while he said nothing, then he raised his blessed head and looked at me as he recited this couplet:
>
> *Why should you go to the mountain? Stay with me.*
> *The mountain is no place of refuge any more.*
>
> A change came over me when I heard these lines. I said to myself: "If the venerable Khwāja recited this couplet for my sake, let him repeat it." The Khwāja then turned to me and quoted the verse again,

*The spelling of this name is uncertain. The form Ūbahī may be more correct.

> mentioning that it was by Shaikh Kamāl Khūjandī and addressing me by name.

Straight after this, Khwāja 'Ubaidallāh left the school, mounted his horse and rode away. Abū Sa'īd was drawn to him so powerfully that he felt "dazed and confused." He wondered how the Khwāja could have known his name and how he could have chosen such a relevant couplet. Leaving all his books and things to his college friends, he entered the service of 'Ubaidallāh Aḥrār and embarked on the spiritual path.

He has much of importance to say about Sufism; for instance:

> What is meant by the spiritual quest is not only to enjoy the rank one has achieved, but to yearn for the stages that lie ahead. For the goal is infinity. In comparison to what still remains unreached, all that has been attained is a mere drop in the ocean. If the traveller leaves this world too easily content, he will be confined eternally to that limited experience, forever deprived of boundless delights and ecstasies.

♦ Mawlānā Muḥammad Qāḍī

Mawlānā Muḥammad Qāḍī was an advanced disciple of Khwāja Aḥrār, whose states and marvelous exploits he described in a work entitled *Silsilat al-'Ārifīn wa-Tadhkirat al-Ṣiddīqīn* (Pedigree of the Sages and Biography of the Saints). According to his statement in this book, he entered the Khwāja's service in the year 885 of the Hijra and continued in that service for twelve years. He had such an aptitude for Sufism that his presence in a group meeting would inspire the teacher to speak of the most profound realities.

As a young man he wanted to take leave of the Khwāja in order that he might go to college in Herāt. It was the summer season and he found the Khwāja writing in a corner of the garden. When he saw Mawlānā Qāḍī, the venerable 'Ubaidallāh got up, took the young man by the hand, and led him to a quiet spot.

"As soon as the Khwāja's hand touched mine," he tells us, "I was lost to myself. When I had recovered my normal consciousness after a while, he said: 'I don't suppose you can read my handwriting.' Then he took a piece of writing from his blessed pocket and read it to me. When he had finished reading, he folded the paper and gave it to me, saying: 'Take good care of my letter.'"

The text of the letter is given in the *Rashaḥāt:*

> The true essence of worship is humble veneration, supplication, and contrition. These qualities arise in the heart through the contemplation of God's glorious majesty. The achievement of such bliss depends on love. Love becomes manifest through obedience to the Prophet and Master of all ages. We therefore need to know how to obey.
>
> Thus it becomes necessary to pay attention to those scholars who are the heirs to true religious knowledge. As for those who abuse their learning, making it a means to worldly gain or an instrument of fame and fortune, they must be avoided.
>
> One should not mix with dervishes who indulge in music and dancing and who do not hesitate to buy and sell all kinds of things. One's ears must be deaf to heretical doctrines. One must study to acquire true wisdom, in conformity with the practice of the Prophet.
>
> May you be blessed with peace . . .

After the letter had been handed over, they rejoined the other disciples. Mawlānā Muḥammad Qaḍī received the Khwāja's permission to go to Herāt and a blessing was recited. Qāḍī Muḥammad encountered so many hardships and obstacles on his journey that he finally lost the desire to study. He returned to Samarqand and devoted himself to the service of Khwāja 'Ubaidallāh.

♦ Mawlānā Khwāja 'Alī Tashkandī

Mawlānā Khwāja 'Alī Tashkandī was one of the earliest disciples. Khwāja 'Alī was only twenty-one when Khwāja Aḥrār came back from Khurāsān to his native Tashkent and took up agriculture. Even at that time he was in the service of Khwāja Aḥrār.

♦ Shaikh Ḥabīb Najjār Tashkandī

Shaikh Ḥabīb Najjār Tashkandī was a business agent and a faithful disciple of Khwāja Aḥrār.

♦ Mawlānā Nūr al-Dīn Tashkandī

Mawlānā Nūr al-Dīn Tashkandī was one of those who "won approval and admiration" and is known to have been bound to Khwāja Aḥrār by very strong ties of affection. He died at a very early age, having saved Khwāja Aḥrār by taking upon himself a serious illness that had afflicted the Khwāja.* The year of his death was 840 by the Islamic reckoning. It seems he was a very comely youth.

♦ Mawlānā Zāda Otrārī

Mawlānā Zāda Otrārī, whose personal name was Muḥammad ibn 'Abdallāh, seems to have been a great friend and close companion of Khwāja Aḥrār. He kept the company of Khwāja Abū Naṣr-i Parsā.

He was so talented that Khwāja Aḥrār considered it unnecessary to his progress to undergo training in dhikr. Before presenting himself to Khwāja Aḥrār, he had served an order of Turkish shaikhs called the 'Ishqiyya (Turkish *Ashkiler*). He was given to rapture and ecstasy. He went on Pilgrimage during the Khwāja's lifetime, and on his return he settled in Damascus, where he engaged in spiritual teaching until his death.

According to the *Nafaḥāt,* 'Ubaidallāh al-Aḥrār said: "I never met anyone with the learning and devotion of Mawlānā Zāda Otrārī." He is famous for having achieved "perfect renunciation and abstraction from the world."

♦ Mawlānā Nāṣir al-Dīn Otrārī

Mawlānā Nāṣir al-Dīn Otrārī, the young brother of Mawlānā Zāda, spent a long time in the service of Khwāja Aḥrār after the latter had captivated his heart.

---

*Editor's note: On page 114 a similar story is attributed to Mawlānā Qāsim. This text reflects the original.

♦ Hindū Khwāja Turkistānī

Hindū Khwāja Turkistānī, a favorite companion of Khwāja Aḥrār, was a Turkestani prince and had been a young knight. We learn from the *Rashaḥāt* that he was originally hostile and antagonistic to Khwāja Aḥrār, but became his servant and disciple when the Khwāja worked a miracle. "He was a strikingly handsome young man." Traces of ecstasy and rapture were apparent in his face.

♦ Mawlānā Ismā'īl Firhatī

Mawlānā Ismā'īl Firhatī was the youngest son of Mawlānā Saif al-Dīn Mannārī, a companion of the venerable Bahā' al-Dīn Naqshband. A senior friend and companion of Khwāja 'Ubaidallāh, he is said to have been a scholar and a person of great worth. The venerable Khwāja loved and respected him both for his own abilities and for his father's sake.

At their first meeting, Khwāja Aḥrār offered Mawlānā Ismā'il a bunch of Ḥusaynī grapes. Such spiritual grace was present at that moment that Mawlānā Ismā'īl experienced a state of absence and non-being and the grapes fell from his hand. From the instant he recovered consciousness he became the Khwāja's inseparably devoted servant. After the Khwāja's death, he went to Mecca and settled in the Sanctuary there for the rest of his life.

Apart from the twenty already mentioned, the venerable Khwāja Aḥrār had twelve other well-known companions. According to the *Thamarāt al-Fu'ād,* they were: Shaikh A'yān Kāzarūnī, Shaikh Raḥmatallāh, Mawlānā Sulṭān 'Alī, Mawlānā Mūsā, Mawlānā Najm al-Dīn, 'Abd al-Wahhāb Samarqandī, 'Abdallāh Sirmakī, Khwāja Muḥammad Amīn Bulghārī, Mīr Qinād Harawī, Khwāja Muṣṭafā Rūmī, Fakhr al-Dīn 'Alī Wā'iẓ, Ismā'īl Shīrwānī.

Khwāja Aḥrār had three other associates named Ismā'īl: Mawlānā Ismā'īl Qamarī, Mawlānā Ismā'īl Shamsī, and Mawlānā Ismā'īl Thālith. The last of these was a scientist and scholar, who had read nearly all the important literature existing at that time. His talents were recognized by Khwāja 'Ubaidallāh when he came from Herāt to Samarqand to join his service.

♦ The Spread of Khwāja Aḥrār's Influence to Anatolia

Also important are two figures who came under the Khwāja's spiritual influence in Samarqand before emigrating to the Ottoman Empire: Shaikh Ilāhī and Sayyid Amīr Aḥmad al-Bukhārī. As heirs to the tradition of the Masters, they gave the Naqshbandī Order a new lease of life in Anatolia and the Balkans.

♦ Shaikh Faḍlī Ilāhī

The first name of Shaikh Faḍlī Ilāhī was 'Abdallāh. He was born in Simav (near Kütahya) in the province of Germiyān. After devoting himself for some time to exoteric studies at the Zeyrek College in Istanbul, he accompanied the learned Mawlānā Ṭūsī to Khurāsān and furthered his education there.

Having developed an interest in Sufism, he sold his books and went to Samarqand, where Khwāja 'Ubaidallāh Aḥrār admitted him into his service. After receiving instruction and training in the disciplines of the Order, he was given permission by the Khwāja to spend a year in Bukhārā, at the mausoleum of Khwāja Bahā' al-Dīn Naqshband, where he underwent nine successive forty-day retreats. Very few dervishes had ever been capable of achieving such a feat. According to the *Nafaḥāt,* "Completely sustained by the noble spirit of the venerable Khwāja, he solved all his problems and received spiritual grace and blessings."

As we read in the same source, it was Shaikh Ilāhī who introduced the Way of the Masters to Anatolia, Istanbul, and the Balkans. Invited to settle in Istanbul, he took up residence in a small apartment in the school attached to the Zeyrek Mosque. There he gave teaching and instruction in the Way of the Masters to all who came as seekers, including many great and famous men.

After some time, he grew weary of the pressures that went with being a celebrity. Leaving Sayyid Aḥmad al-Bukhārī to take his place, he accepted the invitation of Ghāzī Evranosoghlu Aḥmad Bey, a great Governor of Rumelia, and moved to Vardar Yenijesi. There he spent the rest of his days as a spiritual teacher and author, dying in the year 896/1490. His works include *Zād al-Mushtaqīn* and *Najāt al-Arwāḥ*. His tomb is in Yenije.

♦ Sayyid Aḥmad al-Bukhārī

A native of Bukhārā, he was a direct descendant of the venerable Imām Ḥusayn. He joined Khwāja Aḥrār in Samarqand and spent many years in his service. According to the *Nafaḥāt,* Sayyid Aḥmad felt uncomfortable about the excessive honor, respect, and attention shown to him by Khwāja Aḥrār.

Khwāja 'Ubaidallāh apologized for this one day, saying: "How can I fail to show you great respect? Whenever I look at you I see the majesty of two noble men, for you are descended from the Messenger of Allāh and Khwāja Maḥmūd Faghnawī is your grandfather."

To escape this embarrassing reverence and attention, Sayyid Bukhārī migrated to Anatolia together with Shaikh Ilāhī. The venerable Shaikh regarded him as his closest companion and would let no one come between them.

With Shaikh Ilāhī's permission, he left Simav to go on Pilgrimage to Mecca. He spent some time in Jerusalem and stayed for a whole year in Mecca the Ennobled. In the following year the shaikh sent him a message with some merchants who were going on Pilgrimage. He accepted the invitation and returned to Simav and the service of the shaikh.

He tells us in his own words:

> I stayed in Simav with the venerable shaikh. He used to make me lead the five ritual prayers each day in the convent. At sunrise I would set off for the mountain, where I cut firewood all morning. After leading the midday prayers, I would plough or reap according to the season. At other times I would fetch loads of brushwood on my back, using it to mend the fences round the shaikh's orchard garden. After leading the afternoon prayers, I would be once again in the shaikh's presence and at his service.*

**Nafaḥāt.*

A disciple of Shaikh Ilāhī, called Muṣliḥ al-Dīn Khalīfa, tells us: "I heard the venerable shaikh himself say: 'For six years at Simav, Amīr Bukhārī always preserved his ritual purity from the late evening prayer till he led us in prayer the next dawn.' He would doze for an hour against a tree on his way to the mountain." Muṣlīh al-Dīn heard from Sayyid Bukhārī personally that this was all the sleep he ever took.

When Shaikh Faḍlī Ilāhī died in Yenije, Sayyid Bukhārī emerged as his successor in Istanbul. He was well liked by people of all classes, who attained felicity in his service. He used to give guidance and instruction to seekers in an unpretentious building he had constructed.

> To cope with the multitude of seekers, it later became necessary to build a mosque and many rooms in a place near the Balat district, overlooking Galata. Pious foundations were endowed for the maintenance of these institutions and to provide for the food and expenses of resident dervishes. Let us hope that those chambers remain occupied and illuminated by sincere seekers and faithful aspirants as long as this world endures.*

His method of spiritual work included forsaking formalities and ceremonies; constant divine remembrance privately performed; seclusion from the crowd; taking little sleep and little food, keeping vigil by night and fasting by day.

He shunned heretical innovations and kept the world at bay. Worldly matters were never discussed at his meetings. He had little in the way of exoteric learning, yet when the Qur'ān was recited in his presence he would give three or four hidden meanings, if not more.

He died in Istanbul in the year 922/1516. According to the *Nafaḥāt,* there was an eclipse of the moon on the night of his death. He had reached the age of seventy-three.

His mausoleum is in a sorry state of disrepair. It is situated in the Fātiḥ quarter of Istanbul, on a street that bears his name.

**Nafaḥāt.*

The Renowned Mawlānā 'Abd al-Raḥmān Jāmī

One of the greatest Sufis of Islam to emerge in the ninth/fifteenth century, Mawlānā 'Imād al-Dīn 'Abd al-Raḥmān Nūr al-Dīn Jāmī was born at Jām in the province of Khurāsān on 23 Sha'bān 817/1414. He lived to the age of eighty-one and died in Herāt in 898/1492.

He traced his descent from Imām Muḥammad al-Shaibānī, the "Second Imām" and famous disciple of the Supreme Imām, Abū Ḥanīfa. His father was Mawlānā Niẓām al-Dīn Aḥmad Dashtī, who was renowned for his learning and piety. The surname Dashtī refers to the quarter of Iṣfahān where he lived before moving in the course of events to the province of Jām.

It was in the year of Mawlānā Jāmī's birth that Sultan Shāhrukh achieved great conquests in Iraq and Iran.

According to the *Nafaḥāt al-Uns:*

> His own noble name is 'Abd al-Raḥmān, while his father's is Aḥmad. He tells us in his own words how he came to choose Jāmī as his pen name: "My birthplace is Jām. What drips from my pen is a drop from the cup [*jām*] of the Shaikh al-Islām. Hence my *nom de plume* in the poets' register is Jāmī."
>
> Jām, in the province of Khurāsān, is the birthplace of Shaikh al-Islām Aḥmad al-Nāmiq al-Jāmī. Mawlānā Jāmī died in the year 898 of the Hijra. His blessed tomb is in Herāt.

They say that, during the Kizilbash interregnum and the occupation of Herāt, the Mullah's son disinterred his body and took it for safety to another province. Finding the tomb empty, the Kizilbash invaders set fire to the tree that grew nearby.

The venerable Mullah received his initiation from Khwāja Sa'd al-Dīn Kāshgharī, but he spent more time in the company of Khwāja 'Ubaidallāh Aḥrār. In dedicating his works to the venerable Khwāja, he declares his devotion and affection toward him. He also associated with many other shaikhs.

He was a man of great virtue and an outstanding scholar. So widely renowned were his wisdom and learning that the Ottoman Sultan (Mehmed the Conqueror) sent emissaries to invite him to his court. He also corresponded with the Emperor of India. His writings bear witness to the exceptional elegance of his style. He wrote many books and treatises, in prose and in verse, all of them prized for their wisdom and grace.

He produced three collections of poetry and gave responses to the classical odes. He had a marvelous poetic style and is famous for his rhetoric and eloquence. He wrote many works on the science of Reality and the mysteries of Sufism, including a commentary on some of the odes of Ibn Fāriḍ and an interpretation of the *Fuṣūṣ,* entitled *Naqsh al-Fuṣūṣ*. Short but useful are his treatises on semantics, rhyme, and prosody, the art of poetry, and arithmetic. His commentary on the first chapters of the Qur'ān is in Arabic. It contains a complete explanation of the Opening Sūra. I [Lâmiî Chelebi, the Turkish translator of the *Nafaḥāt*] am making a translation of his work on the *Shawāhid al-Nubūwa* (Signs of Prophecy). In a word, his learning is infinite and impossible to describe. In a book entitled *Silsilat al-Dhahab* (The Chain of Gold) he gives an incisive account of the various sects and their doctrines, distinguishing clearly between Truth and falsehood.

♦ Mawlānā Jāmī's Education

Having gone with his father to Herāt, the young Mawlānā Jāmī became a student at the Niẓāmiyya School near the Iraq Gate. In Arabic language and the methodology of Islamic science his teacher was the famous Mawlānā Junaid al-Uṣūlī. It took him only forty days to learn all he needed to know from Mawlānā Khwāja Samarqandī, a prominent disciple of Sayyid Sharīf Jurjānī and a leading research scholar. While still in Herāt, he spent much time attending the lectures of Mawlānā Muḥammad Shihāb al-Dīn, a scholar in the line of Sa'd al-Dīn Taftāzānī. When he moved to Samarqand, he became a respected student of Qāḍī Zāda Rūmī.

According to the *Rashaḥāt* Qāḍī Zāda once said of him: "Since the founding of Samarqand, no one with such natural and spiritual talents has ever crossed to this side of the Oxus."

One day in Herāt the famous astronomer and mathematician 'Alī Kushchu came to a lecture and asked some very difficult questions about astronomy. Quite spontaneously, without pausing to think, the venerable Jāmī gave a full and definitive answer to each question. 'Alī Kushchu was dumbfounded. He would later tell his own pupils: "From that day I understand that holy inspiration is still at work here in this world."

Because of the power of his intellect, Mawlānā Jāmī found it possible to come at the top of his class every time, even without studying very hard. In the exoteric field, he quickly caught up with and then surpassed his professors.

Mawlānā Jāmī once said of his professors: "Not one of them is entitled to consider himself my teacher. I am really my father's pupil, since it was from him I learned the language."

It was during his student days that three of his friends insisted on taking Jāmī along with them on some errand to the office of one of Shāhrukh's ministers. They waited a long time at the minister's door but could not obtain an audience. For the rest of his life, the venerable Jāmī would never call upon men of worldly importance.

♦ His Sufi Initiation

Before and after prayers each day, Mawlānā Sa'd al-Dīn Kāshgharī used to sit chatting with his disciples at the gate of the Herāt Mosque. Mawlānā Jāmī's regular path led past the Mosque and Sa'd al-Dīn Kāshgharī would say, each time he walked by: "That is a very talented young man. He seems to have captivated my heart, but I don't know how to catch him."

At that time Mawlānā Jāmī became infatuated with a young beauty. In an effort to rid himself of this obsession, he left Herāt and went to Samarqand. One night, the venerable Kāshgharī appeared to him in a dream and said, "Come, brother. Find a loved one you can never leave." Greatly affected by this vision, Jāmī went straight back to Khurāsān. He had a natural inclination toward Sufism, into which he was now initiated by Sa'd al-Dīn Kāshgharī. Sa'd al-Dīn said at that time: "Today a falcon has been caught in our net. God, Exalted is He, has made me happy by sending me this young Jāmī."

One of Jāmī's college professors, Mawlānā Shihāb al-Dīn Jājurmī, said in this connection: "For the first time in five hundred years a real scholar has emerged on the soil of Khurāsān, only to run off after Sa'd al-Dīn Kāshgharī."

When he had abandoned his formal education to embark on the Sufi path, Jāmī began a program of rigorous spiritual exercises prescribed for him by Sa'd al-Dīn Kāshgharī. He became extremely reclusive, spending all his time in solitary meditation. After this phase, he found it very difficult to express himself in conversation with ordinary people. The words he needed came to him only with great effort. This condition persisted for some time before it gradually disappeared.

Jāmī tells us in his own words: "At the beginning, I used to see visions of light. On the orders of Mawlānā Sa'd al-Dīn, I rejected these visions until they ceased to appear. Visions, illuminations, and marvels are not to be encouraged. The most marvelous experience a dervish can have is to achieve ecstasy in perfect communion and so escape from himself for a while."

They once asked him: "How is it that some of us receive mystic revelations, while others have no access to those realms?" He gave this explanation: "There are two ways of pursuing the spiritual quest. One is by traditionally transmitted training, which leads the seeker back to his source by retracing the path that brought him down into the world of manifestation. The other is the special way of the Masters, on which the traveller directs himself exclusively toward the Divine Essence."

♦ The Sufis He Met

He was a five-year-old child when he met the venerable Khwāja Muḥammad Parsā, who passed through the province of Jām on his Pilgrimage to Mecca. Sixty years later he would still recall the radiance he had seen in Khwāja Parsā's countenance.

In his childhood he also received the blessing of Mawlānā Fakhr al-Dīn Lūristānī. He met Khwāja Burhān al-Dīn Abū Naṣr-i Parsā and sat in the company of Shaikh Bahā' al-Dīn 'Umar and Khwāja Shams al-Dīn Muḥammad Gawsūyī. When he attended one of the latter's meetings, the Khwāja found himself uttering profound truths without premeditation. Referring to Mullah Jāmī, he said: "A light has been rekindled in our meeting today."

Khwāja Shams al-Dīn is said to have been a great believer in the works of the venerable Muḥyī-l Dīn ibn al-'Arabī. He used to speak about the Supreme Shaikh's monistic system in such terms that even literal-minded scholars could find no objection. While preaching, he would sometimes give a cry and go into ecstasy, communicating this state to the whole congregation.

Mawlānā Jāmī also had long associations with Jalāl al-Dīn Abū Yazīd Pūrānī and Mawlānā Shams al-Dīn Muḥammad Asad.

♦ Mawlānā Jāmī's Meetings with Khwāja Aḥrār

Mawlānā Jāmī met Khwāja 'Ubaidallāh Aḥrār on four occasions. Two of these encounters were in Samarqand, the third in Herāt, and the fourth in Merv. According to Mawlānā Ḥusain, author of the *Rashaḥāt,* the venerable Jāmī jotted this note in the margin of a book: "It was in the vicinity of Merv that the venerable Khwāja 'Ubaidallāh asked me how old I was. When I told him my age was approximately fifty-five, he said: 'In that case, I am twelve years older than you.'"

Mawlānā Jāmī had great faith in the venerable Khwāja 'Ubaidallāh and was very fond of him. They corresponded with each other frequently, both before and after their meetings, and Mawlānā Jāmī's notes and letters bear witness to his esteem and affection for the Khwāja.

Mawlānā Jāmī went thrice to Samarqand. The first journey was made in the time of Mīrzā Ulugh Bey, when he went to study under Qaḍī Zāda Rūmī. His second trip was for the purpose of meeting Khwāja Aḥrār. He made a note of the date: Muḥarram 870. On the third occasion, in 874, he set out to meet Khwāja Aḥrār in Samarqand, but encountered him on the road. The Khwāja was on his way to Turkestan, in the hope of effecting a reconciliation between 'Umar Shaikh Mīrzā and Sultan Aḥmad Mīrzā, the sons of Sultan Abū Sa'īd Mīrzā. They stayed together for three days, then Khwāja 'Ubaidallāh sent Mawlānā Jāmī and his own companions to Fārāb, while he went on to Turkestan. After reconciling the two brothers, the Khwāja returned to Tashkent, fetching Jāmī and the others from Fārāb to participate in meetings and gatherings over a period of several days.

According to the *Rashaḥāt,* it was reported by Abū Sa'īd Awbahī, a disciple of the Khwāja's who attended these meetings, that the venerable Jāmī and Aḥrār spent most of their time together in silent communion. Khwāja 'Ubaidallāh said something now and then.

One day Mawlānā Jāmī mentioned that he had some problems with Ibn al-'Arabī's *al-Futūḥāt al-Makkiyya,* which even careful reading and reflection had failed to resolve. Khwāja Aḥrār sent for a copy of the book, then Jāmī pointed out the most difficult passages, and they read them together. According to the *Rashaḥāt:*

> The venerable Khwāja said: "Leave the book alone for a moment, while I make some preliminary remarks." He then proceeded to give

> a detailed introduction to the work, saying many unusual and surprising things. At length he said: "Now let us turn to the book again." When he opened the book, the meaning proved to be perfectly obvious in the light of his previous clarification.

These conversations in Tashkent went on for fifteen days, at the end of which time Mullah Jāmī returned to Samarqand. He described the sayings of Khwāja 'Ubaidallāh as sweeter than those of any other Master. The venerable Aḥrār directed many seekers to Jāmī, commending him highly. Mawlānā Ḥusain Ṣafī tells of a dream in which the venerable 'Ubaidallāh appeared to him and said: "How strange that people should come to Transoxiana [i.e., to himself], when the ocean of light [meaning Mullah Jāmī] is making waves in Khurāsān."

Khwāja Aḥrār also used to say: "If someone has seen Mawlānā 'Abd al-Raḥmān Jāmī in Khurāsān, why should he need to cross the Oxus?"

Unlike other Shaikhs and Masters, Jāmī did not take on pupils. When people wondered about this, 'Ubaidallāh Aḥrār used to say: "Let me tell you the advice of Khwāja 'Abd al-Khāliq Ghujdawānī: 'Close the door of shaikhhood and open the door of friendship. Close the door of solitude and open the door of companionship.'"

Mawlānā Jamī would never instruct people in the practice of dhikr, but if a genuine seeker came along he would tell him about the spiritual path. He used to say: "The burden of shaikhhood is more than I can bear."

♦ His Pilgrimage to Mecca

He set out on Pilgrimage in the month of Rabī'u-l'awwal 877/1472, starting from Herāt and passing through Nīshāpūr, Sabzvār, Bisṭām, Simnān, Qazvīn, and Hamadān. At Hamadān the Mawlānā was welcomed with a great display of honor and affection by the ruler, Minūchahr Shāh, who entertained his entire caravan for three days, providing royal banquets during their stay. On their departure he detailed a troop of soldiers to escort them in safety from Kurdistan to the frontiers of Baghdād.

The venerable Jāmī reached Baghdād in the middle of the month of Jumādā-l'ākhira and went to visit the tomb of the venerable Imām Ḥusain at Karbalā'.

While in Baghdād, Jāmī became involved in a dispute arising out of a misinterpretation of some verses in his work *Silsilat al-Dhahab.* In response to the provocation of Shī'ī extremists, a debate was held in one of the city's great colleges. Before a select audience of scholars, Mawlānā Jāmī succeeded in silencing his critics. After this episode, which concluded a four-month stay in Baghdād, the caravan moved on. The journey was broken again at Najaf, for a visit to the mausoleum of the venerable Imām 'Alī ibn Abī Ṭālib, may Allāh be pleased with him.

Medina was reached on 22 or 23 Dhū-l Ḥijja. After a visit to the resting place of the blessed Messenger, the caravan completed its journey to Mecca. The rites of Pilgrimage were duly performed, then they returned to Medina after a sojourn of fifteen days.

It was at this time that the venerable Jāmī composed his famous lyric poem, which may be translated:

To the Ka'ba I came and there I discovered Your
fragrance.
As I beheld the beauty of the Ka'ba, I saw Your
countenance.
As I witnessed the Ka'ba draped in black, to Your black
locks I stretched my hands.

On the return journey they stopped in Damascus for forty-five days, while Jāmī studied Prophetic Tradition with the great scholar Qaḍī Muḥammad Ḥaḍrawī. At Aleppo he was received with honor and respect by the local nobles and notables.

News of Mullah Jāmī's travels reached the Ottoman Sultan Mehmed, who had conquered Istanbul (the former Constantinople) some twenty years earlier. According to the *Rashaḥāt,* he dispatched emissaries to Jāmī in the company of Khwāja 'Aṭā'allāh Kirmānī, an old friend of the Mawlānā's, "sending him five thousand gold pieces for his expenses and promising many thousands of florins in addition, if he would be so gracious as to visit his domains for a few days."

As it turned out, however, some "divine inspiration" had prompted the venerable Jāmī to leave Damascus for Aleppo a few days before the ambassadors arrived. When news of their arrival reached him in Aleppo, the venerable Mawlānā waited to see if they would follow him there, "lest there be a failure to obey the command of a mighty sovereign." Then he set off in the direction of Tabrīz. The route through Kurdistan was more hazardous than ever at that time, since the Ottomans were at war with the Eastern Turks. But a Turkmen chieftain named Muḥammad Bey was a great believer in the venerable Jāmī. He provided an escort of three hundred cavalrymen, who saw the caravan safely through to Tabrīz.

The venerable Jāmī received a warm and respectful welcome in Tabrīz. Declining the pressing invitation of Uzun Ḥasan, the ruler of Azerbaijan, with the excuse that he must hurry back to his aged mother, he set off for Khurāsān and reached Herāt on Friday, 18 Sha'bān 878/1473. His homecoming was an occasion of rejoicing on the part of all the nobles and notables, including Sultan Ḥusain Bāiqarā and 'Alī Shīrnavāyī. Following his Pilgrimage journey, the venerable Mawlānā led a secluded life in Herāt, producing many important literary works during this period.

♦ Some Sayings

The following are excerpted from among the many recorded by his brother-in-law, Mawlānā Ḥusain Ṣafī, the author of the *Rashaḥāt:*

> According to the Masters of Reality, true nobility is not a matter of being descended from a prince or statesman. Genuine nobility is an essential quality inherent in a person's character.

He once asked someone what he was doing. "I am in repose," the man replied. "I have stepped aside from the temptations of the world and am sitting in the corner of contentment and ease." When Jāmī heard this, he said: "Wrapping yourself up in a corner is not peace and well-being. To enjoy well-being you must be saved from your own selfhood. Once that has been achieved, you may sit in a quiet nook or mix with other people, as you may choose."

An odor of neglect is emitted by a seeker who has not experienced sorrow and contrition, while the perfume of peace and composure issues from one who is sad and contrite. Those associated with the Masters of Wisdom generally bear the marks of sadness and contrition.

Essential affection is loving for no reason. Such an affection for the Divine Truth is called Essential affection. This is the highest degree of affection. If love comes with kindness and goes with unkindness, it is not Essential affection.

When someone asked him why he seldom used the technical language of Sufism, he said: "That would be all very well if we wished to deceive each other for a while, turning a subject of real importance into a verbal plaything."

The words of the saints are taken from the lamp niche of the Reality-of-Muḥammad. These holy words deserve to be accorded the same respect as the Qur'ān and the Prophetic Traditions.

Old age is the final consequence of youth. The way we spend our youth comes to be written on our faces in old age.

Someone once asked our teacher, Sa'd al-Dīn Kāshgharī: "Teach me something to which I can devote the rest of my life." Mawlānā Sa'd al-Dīn put his hand over his heart, saying: "Attend to this; this is what work is all about."

Mawlānā Jāmī was a cheerful person and his conversation was full of wit and humor. Some of his witty remarks are included in a collection called *Laṭā'if al-Ṭawā'if,* made in 939/1532 by Jāmī's brother-in-law Mawlānā 'Alī Ḥusain. A couple of examples:

A poet once boasted in his presence: "I have given the answer to the poetic works of Kamāl Khujandī and Ḥāfiẓ of Shīrāz, as well as to the hundred sayings of Imām 'Alī." The venerable Jāmī asked him: "And what answer will you give to God?"

Another poet said: "I went to the Ka'ba and rubbed my poetry collection against the Black Stone to increase its value." Said Mullah Jāmī: "It would have been more appropriate if you had plunged it in the Zamzam Well."

Like the noble Mathnawī (Mesnevi), Jāmī's own works are rich in funny stories.

♦ The Works of Mawlānā Jāmī

The following works, mostly on Sufi topics, were mainly composed in the latter part of his life:

Fātiḥat al-Shabāb: His first collection of poems. Printed in Istanbul, 1284/1868.

Wāsiṭat al-'Iqd: His second collection of poems, completed ten years after the first.

Khātimat al-Ḥayāt: His third collection of poems. Written two years after the second.

Haft Avrang: An imitative work, based on Niẓāmī's five tales told in verse (*Panj Ganj*). It consists of seven books: 1. *Silsilat al-Dhahab* (The Chain of Gold); 2. *Salāmān wa-Absāl;* 3. *Tuḥfat al-Aḥrār;* 4. *Ṣubḥat al-Asrār;* 5. *Yūsuf wa-Zulaikha;* 6. *Lailā wa-Majnūn*; 7. *Khurdnāma-i Iskandarī.*

Silsilat al-Dhahab: 7,200 couplets on philosophical and religious themes. Dedicated to Ḥusain Bāiqarā.

Salāmān wa-Absāl: A version of the biblical story of Solomon and Absalom.

Tuḥfat al-Aḥrār: A work in imitation of Niẓāmī's *Makhzan al-Asrār,* dealing with ethics and theology. There are two commentaries on it in Turkish.

Ṣubḥat al-Asrār: Poems in the same vein as the above.

Yūsuf wa-Zulaikha: A poetic account of the love story of the Prophet Joseph, on him be peace, and Zulaikha, the wife of Potiphar.

Lailā wa-Majnūn: A love story in verse, reminiscent of Niẓāmī's famous work of the same name. Like many other poets, Jāmī takes a mystical view of love and beauty, separation and reunion. There is a French translation by Chézy.

Khurdnāma-i Iskandarī: The last of the seven books collectively entitled *Haft Avrang.* It gives the Islamic legend of Alexander the Great, relating his travels in search of the fountain of wisdom. Translated into German, French, and Turkish.

Nafaḥāt al-Uns: Spiritual biographies of Islamic Sufis. This is Jāmī's most famous work. Widely read and referred to as a principal source for the study of Islamic mysticism. Translated into Ottoman Turkish by Lâmiî Chelebi of Bursa and into Eastern Turkish by 'Alī Shīrnava'ī. Several manuscripts are extant, as well as the printed edition of 1289/1872. Also translated into Arabic, by Tāj al-Dīn Zakariyā.

Bahāristān: Follows the style and content of the *Gulistān* by Sādī of Shīrāz. Jāmī wrote this work in 840 of the Hijra, for his son Ḍiyā' al-Dīn Yūsuf. A mixture of prose and verse, its contents cover Sufism, ethics, politics, love, humor, poetry, and animal tales. Dedicated to Sultan Bāiqarā. Translated into German, English, and French.

Shawāhid al-Nubūwa: Written c. 886/1481. The Turkish translation by Lâmiî Chelebi was printed in Istanbul in 1293/1876 and again in 1958.

Lawā'iḥ: A treatise on the fundamentals and theories of Sufism. Contains Sufistic quatrains (see sample on page 140).

Lawāmi': A Persian commentary on the *Khamriyya* of Ibn al-Fāriḍ (see page 140).

Sharḥ-i Fuṣūṣ al-Ḥikam: A commentary on the famous work of the venerable Muḥyī-l Dīn ibn al-'Arabī.

Naqd al-Nuṣūṣ fī Sharḥ al-Fuṣūṣ: Persian commentary on the abridged version of the *Fuṣūṣ*. Turkish translation published in Istanbul in 1328/1910.

Risālatun fi-lwujūd: Explains the great Ibn al-'Arabī's ideas on the subject of Being.

Risāla-i Taḥqīq: A short account of Sufi methods with a comparison between the theologians and the philosophers of Islam.

Risāla-i Lā ilāha illā-llāh: On the mystical meanings of the affirmation of Divine Unity, according to the Masters of Reality.

Manāqib-i Ḥaḍrat-i Mawlawī: A spiritual biography of Mawlānā (Mevlânâ) Jalāl al-Dīn Rūmī.

Sukhanān-i Khwāja Parsā: Contains the sayings of the great Master Khwāja Muḥammad Parsā.

Manāqib-i Shaikh al-Islām Khwāja 'Abdallāh al-Anṣārī: Spiritual biography of 'Abdallāh al-Anṣārī, who is famous for his supplications and quatrains.

In addition to the works above, Jāmī produced treatises on such subjects as the Qur'ān, Prophetic Tradition, Sufism, literature, music, poetry, and rhyme. He also wrote a popular manual of Arabic grammar, which schoolboys used to call "Mullah Jāmī."

All told, Mawlānā 'Abd al-Raḥmān Jāmī has nearly forty compositions to his credit. Judging by the specimens of his handwriting preserved in the Leningrad Library, he must have been a superb calligrapher.

♦ Selections from His Works

♦ Poetry

You and only You, concealed, revealed; a fool am I.
You inside the heart, You inside the soul; a fool am I.
Everywhere I looked for You, when "Everywhere" is You;
a fool am I.

♦ ♦ ♦

I turned the pages of the universe and read it like a book.
God and His works I saw there—nothing else, however I might look.

God's being is an ocean; it does not wax, it does not wane.
The waves on its surface are the changing world, not for two seconds the same.

How much longer all this talk of physics and geometry?
Have you much more to say about geology, zoology, and botany?
There are no "substances." One single Essence is the sole Reality,
His works and attributes the sources of this apparent multiplicity.

This universe is but a fleeting dream, or so the silly sophists say.
A dream it is indeed, but one in which Reality forever manifests itself at every moment, night and day.

In all the cosmos but one single Light exists.
That Light shines forth in all appearances.
God is the Light and His manifestations are the universe.
This is the truth of Unity, the rest is vain illusion.

Do not seek true meaning in verbal formulations.
You must look beyond what is relative, with all its limitations.
If, as you say, you wish to find the remedy for ignorance,
Do not look for the key to salvation in outer indications.

♦ ♦ ♦

Objects are vessels of colored glass, struck by the sunlight (of Being).
If the glass is yellow, red, or green, the sun will appear in those colors.

My heart is outside the frontiers of the universe, beyond all its dimensions.
My heart is far from the shadows of the attributes; it mirrors the manifestations of Essence.

I am nothing. Even less than nothing am I.
From one who is nothing, what but nothingness can you expect?
If I speak of the secrets of Reality, what have I but words?

Unless the spell of existence is broken, Reality's treasure is out of reach.
Reality is the ocean, words a mere mirage.
A mirage offers no satisfaction to one who is in the sea.

How happy are they who escape from the world of inner and outer!
Both peace of mind and pain of body are by them transcended.
They make their nest in the secret nook of non-existence,
The home of your love and mine.

Before the spheres began to roll, when water, fire, and earth were yet unmingled,
Then was I drunk in memory of You.
Then was I drunk, although as yet there was no trace of wine or vine.

♦ From the Lawā'iḥ

Absolute beauty is God. Every beauty and perfection manifested at the various levels of being is a reflection of the Light of God's Beauty and Perfection. Light is acquired from that Light, and perfection achieved, by those who attain those degrees. The wisdom of the wise is derived from God's wisdom. The seeing of the seer is the fruit of God's Sight.

It is the attributes of the Essence that descend from the universal and absolute realm of Divinity, appearing as manifestations in the particularized and limited realm of humanity.

You must find the way from the part to the whole, turning from limitation toward liberation. But beware of regarding the part as separate from the whole, and beware of missing liberation through falling into limitation.

When one is so invaded by the Being of God that no consciousness of anything but Him remains, that is annihilation [*fanā'*]. To be unconscious even of that unconsciousness is annihilation upon annihilation.

The Reality of God is Being. His Being is not subject to diminution. He is immune from change and variation. He is exempt from multiplicity. He transcends all manifestations. He is unknowable and invisible. He cannot be spoken of in terms of quantity or quality. Everything that is known is known by Him, but He is beyond the grasp of knowledge and awareness.

♦ From the Lawāmi'

In the eternity before all eternity there was God and nothing but God. There was neither Tablet nor Pen. Manifestations and things were still hidden in non-existence. God knew His own Essence and saw His Essential Perfection and Beauty. He knew His own attributes, works, and phenomena, concealed within the Mystery of Ipseity. And a Voice was heard to say: "Allāh has no need of the worlds."

> Then consciousness, brought into motion by the perfection of His names, became a reality and inclined toward manifestation. This is the origin and source of all love and affection . . . All beauty, virtue, and perfection are derivatives of His Perfection and reflections of His Beauty.
>
> Not everyone can be privy to the secrets of Reality. The state of those who follow the mystic path cannot be known by all. These mysteries are guarded by the use of metaphorical words and expressions. The face of spiritual truth is kept veiled from the eyes of the uninitiated.

♦ His Death

According to the *Rashaḥāt,* Mawlānā Jāmī fell ill on Sunday, 13 Muḥarram 898/1492. His illness lasted six days, till his pulse began to weaken at the time of morning prayers on Friday, 18 Muḥarram, and he died during the Call to Friday congregational prayers (about midday).

According to the *Tadhkira* of Dawlat-Shāh, he was in a speechless coma toward the end of his life. 'Alī Shīrnavā'ī tells us that Mawlānā Jāmī was so "exhausted by Divine Love" that he was forced to take to his bed. Shīrnavā'ī hastened to be with him on the eve of his death. He took Jāmī's little son, Ḍiyā' al-Dīn Yūsuf, away from the bedside, then he watched as the venerable Mawlānā surrendered his soul, offering prayers and supplications in the agony of death.

Ḥusain Bāiqarā, the Sultan of Herāt, attended the funeral with all his retinue in mourning garb. He wept for two hours over Mawlānā's body. In the funeral procession, the bier was carried on the shoulders of great statesmen, scholars, and shaikhs. Big crowds gathered for the occasion. The wives of many important men were also present during the rites of burial.

The venerable Jāmī was buried in Herāt, beside his teacher Sa'd al-Dīn Kāshgharī. Twenty days after his death the foundation of his mausoleum was laid in a ceremony attended by Sultan Ḥusain Bāiqāra, as well as all the shaikhs, scholars, nobles, and notables, and a great throng of ordinary folk.

♦ Mawlānā Jāmī's Sons and Companions

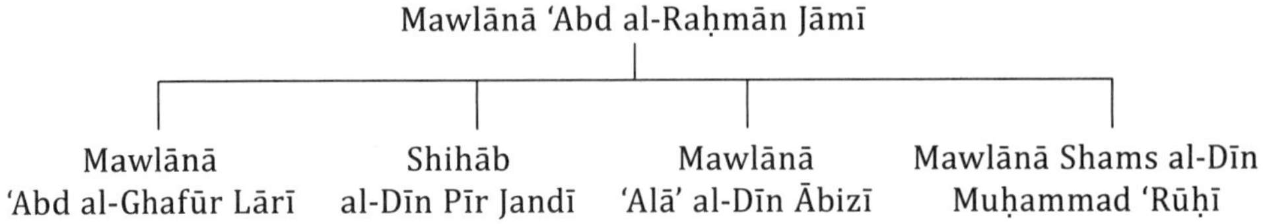

Figure 9

Mawlānā Jāmī married the daughter of Khwāja Gīlān, the eldest son of Sa'd al-Dīn Kāshgharī. He had four sons. The first died when only one day old, before he had been given a name. The second, Ṣafī al-Dīn Muḥammad, lived for one year, while Ẓahīr al-Dīn 'Īsā died after forty days. Jāmī was deeply grieved by the death of Ṣafī al-Dīn, for whom he composed an elegy. His third son, Khwāja Ḍiyā' al-Dīn Yūsuf, was the only one to survive him.

His principal companions were: Mawlānā 'Abd al-Ghafūr Lārī, Shihāb al-Dīn Pīr Jandī, Mawlānā 'Alā' al-Dīn Ābizī, Mawlānā Shams al-Dīn Muḥammad 'Rūḥī.

Some of the venerable Jāmī's sayings have been handed down from these people. For instance: 'Abd al-Ghafūr Lārī came to him one day, complaining about having to mix with common folk. Jāmī said: "We cannot drive God's people from the earth. The aspirant must learn to conduct himself in such a manner that he is not affected by them." According to the *Rashaḥāt,* Jāmī was busy writing the *Nafaḥāt* when this conversation took place. He said: "One or two pages came to be written without my being aware that I was writing them. Perhaps the pen went on out of habit."

♦ Mawlānā 'Alī ibn Ḥusain Ṣafī

Mawlānā 'Alī ibn Ḥusain Ṣafī was the brother-in-law of Mawlānā 'Abd al-Raḥmān Jāmī; that is, the son-in-law of Khwāja Gīlān, eldest son of Sa'd al-Dīn Kāshgharī. He is the author of *Rashaḥāt-i 'Ain al-Ḥayāt,* a blessed and unusual work on Sufism. He treats his subject seriously and avoids superstition. The book gives a remarkably comprehensive account of the beliefs, practices, and spiritual experiences of many important figures in Islamic Sufism.

In this work the author tells us how he came to meet the venerable Khwāja Aḥrār at the end of Dhū-l Qa'da in the Islamic year 889. The Khwāja told him about the marvelous exploits of the Naqshbandī Masters. He also told him many profound truths, "some of which I was fortunate enough to understand." After each conversation, Mawlānā 'Alī Ḥusain made an exact and careful record of all that he had heard.

At the beginning of Rabī'u-l'awwal 893 he had the good fortune to be admitted into the Khwāja's service, but circumstances did not permit him to remain in his company. To ease the pain of separation, he decided to gather all his notes together in a single compilation. Conditions proved unfavorable to the speedy completion of this project, however, and he did not finish the work till sixteen years later, in 909 of the Hijra. To supplement the material he had heard directly from Khwāja Aḥrār and other Masters, he consulted authoritative Sufi literature.

After tracing the spiritual genealogy of earlier Masters, he fulfilled his original purpose by describing the character and accomplishments of the venerable Khwāja Aḥrār.

He expresses the hope that seekers who enjoy reading his book will remember him in their prayers.

Some information about the author himself can be gleaned from the *Rashaḥāt.* He mentions, for instance, that the surname Safī was conferred on him by Mawlānā Jāmī, in memory of the latter's short-lived son Khwāja Ṣafī al-Dīn Muḥammad. We also learn that his marriage was contracted in the presence of Mawlānā Jāmī and his own professor,

Mawlānā Raḍī al-Dīn 'Abd al-Ghafūr. It was forty days after this event that the venerable Jāmī fell ill for the last time. The dying Mawlānā displayed great tenderness toward him, saying: "You have entered the path of the sons of our venerable Saint, Mawlānā Sa'd al-Dīn. Be hopeful of his spiritual protection and treat your heart well, so that your aim may be achieved."

We find additional information about him in *Qāmūs al-'Ālam:* "'Alī ibn Ḥusain al-Wā'iẓ is the son of the famous Ḥusain al-Wā'iẓ, author of *Anwār-i Suhaylī* and other works. He is himself the author of two fine works, entitled *Laṭā'if al-Ẓarā'if* and *Rashaḥāt.* He is better known as 'Alī Wā'iẓ. He died in 939 of the Hijra."

In the literature of Sufism we rarely come across a work free of fables, superstitions, and exaggerations. Mawlānā 'Alī ibn Ḥusain Ṣafī performed an invaluable service in the field of Islamic esotericism, for he steered well clear of those obfuscating peculiarities that give Islamic Sufism a "mythical" flavor. He presented future generations with clear and precise biographies of the great and genuine Sufis who emerged in Turkestan at a most significant period. May Allāh be eternally pleased with him and with his Masters.

APPENDIX I

The Way of Liberation (*Iṭlāq*) in Islamic Sufism

Perception is subjected to the torment of existence; that is, to the material world of creation, which becomes fixed in a person's consciousness between birth and death. Since our original state is non-being, the existing universe inflicts pain on a sensitive individual. Wittingly or unwittingly, we spend our lives trying to escape by breaking loose from matter. This is the motivation and justification of worldly phenomena.

Certain exceptional individuals are not content to accept the conditions of material existence. Instead of wasting their lives on worldly comforts, they seek non-being in self-annihilation, in the Unseen, and pursue salvation from the "dungeon of existence" to the extent of their capacity. Material existence is relative being, illusory consciousness. Non-being is real existence, being awake. It is the secret of "being without being." The existing universe is the totality of potentialities; that is, of sense-perceptibles and intelligibles, whereas non-existence is non-individualization, the absolute mystery. This latter is the goal and the capital of those who seek realization. It is the origin and destination of the worlds of potentiality.

There is no way to achieve this except through annihilation (*fanā'*). Annihilation means leaving relative, material being to attain the real being of non-existence. It is becoming non-existent. It is the way to ecstasy, which is also called the way of realization and the path of liberation and Oneness. Annihilation means, in fact, a heightening of true perception: from the limited toward the pure, from the concrete toward the abstract. In this sense, the stages of annihilation are the same as the degrees of perception, the "presences" of being.

The significant feature of this system is that it is not merely intellectual; it is a process of realization through discovery and direct experience. It is *ḥāl* (state) as opposed to *qāl* (talk).

Mystical ways can be theoretical or practical and real. Gnostic and monistic systems do not go beyond theories, intellectual ideas, and traditional wisdom. Their followers are led through the various stages and degrees without real discovery; they devote themselves to bookish pursuits and discuss the interpretation of myths and dreams.

High-minded seekers do not stop here. When they are sufficiently mature, they meet with a guide and embark on a course of genuine spiritual development.

The seeker of the theoretical phase now becomes an aspirant. The expectations and consolations of the seeker are replaced by the illuminations and progress of verification and realization.

♦ Stages of the Way

The stages of the way of liberation are attained by direct contemplation and firsthand experience. These stages are:

Annihilation of laws (*fanā' al-aḥkām*); that is, the corporeal "presence"
Annihilation of actions (*fanā' al-af'āl*); that is, the spiritual "presence"
Annihilation of attributes (*fanā' al-ṣifāt*); that is, the "presence" of potentiality
Annihilation of the Essence (*fanā' al-dhāt*); that is, the "presence" of Ipseity

These are also called, respectively, the stages of sense-perception, knowledge, relative occultation, and absolute mystery. Other terms may be met with, referring to these same degrees.

This is the direct route by which to escape from cosmic existence. The seeker's first step in annihilation is to leave the corporeal world and reach the realm of knowledge. This is the hardest and longest phase of all. Those who pass through it successfully, achieving realization at the first degree of conscious death, then gain admittance to the spiritual realm. The "objects of knowledge" are directly perceived at this stage.

The second step is annihilation of attributes, which leads to the realm of relative occultation. The "occult substances" are now perceived. At this stage, with the advent of the intermediacy between the visible and the Unseen, the aspirant finds himself midway between being and non-being; he experiences states of divine love.

"Objects of knowledge" and "occult substances" are called "eternal ideas" (*a'yān thābita*), for they are "the realities of potentialities, fixed in the Divine Consciousness."

Annihilation of the Essence is the complete cessation of individualizations, illusions, and manifestations. It is also called non-individualization, absolute occultation, the secret of existence, the mystery of Ipseity, and so on.

When the seeker has made sufficient progress in annihilation, he finds himself in permanent non-being. With the complete extinction of the personal self, the stages of being are also exhausted. Absolute liberation is attained, and realization is consummated.

These stages of progress on the way of realization can also be classified as:

Progress toward God (*sair ilā-llāh*)
Progress in God (*sair fī-llāh*)
Progress beyond God (*sair 'ani-llāh*)

The phase leading up to annihilation is "progress toward God." "Progress in God" occurs during the various stages of annihilation.

The attainment of permanent non-being is called "progress beyond God." This is the beatitude of "as though it had never been."

The way of annihilation is the way of the great Prophets, the venerable Saints, the Masters of Reality and Essential Truth. Those who follow it through to the end are endowed with divine attributes and absolute virtues. They leave the world of appearances and achieve absolute liberation.

♦ Four Basic Practices of the Mystical Path

The stages of annihilation and permanent non-being are reached by following the mystical path. Four basic practices must be observed:

Remembrance (*dhikr*)
Austerity (*riyāḍāt*)
Contrition (*inkisār*)
Fellowship (*ṣuḥba*)

♦ Remembrance

Constant remembrance is the repetition of the Supreme Divine Name: ALLĀH. The repetition is performed with a kind of rhythmic breathing. It is not subject to restrictions as to where or how often it is to be performed. Divine remembrance is the key to the stages of annihilation and permanent non-being. It is one of the most important techniques for achieving complete inner purification.

As man is in fact the "comprehensive entity," he contains all the levels of Divine Truth and creation and is the bearer of all names. In order to activate this endowment and develop its latent capacity, the aspirant must begin his endeavor by practicing constant remembrance. Unflagging perseverance is demanded of him if he is to succeed in making contact with the Essence.

This is genuine remembrance. It brings inner freedom and deliverance from delusions and superstitious obsessions. It enables one to penetrate the veils. It removes the obstacles that bar our way to absolute liberation. It dissolves complexities and obscurities, making everything clear and simple. It provides a safeguard against deviations. By ensuring an aptitude for austerity, it opens the way to the evolution of being. It puts one in touch with the inner realities. It leads from potentiality to necessity, from existence to non-existence. In other words, it brings one to true poverty.

Apart from the prayers enjoined by religion, this remembrance makes all other invocations and litanies redundant, for the Name of Divine Majesty includes them all.

♦ Austerity

This means constant and rigorous fasting, observed to the extent of our physical capacity. It reduces the need for sleep and talking. It gives rise to a genuine detachment and isolation from the world. By means of fasting, the aspirant achieves wakefulness and alertness. It makes a significant contribution to inner progress.

Hunger is the bread of the Prophets, the dainty morsel of the Saints. It is a divine favor and a grace that is not bestowed on every seeker. Its value is fully appreciated by the Masters of Bliss.

Austerity is the true bond of union. Ardent yearning and innate disposition are passive connections. Hunger is the spur to progress, the active connection that carries us forward stage by stage. All other connections are relative and illusory, unreliable and ineffective, sometimes even harmful.

♦ Contrition

At the appropriate time and according to his ability to bear it, the Supreme Truth places the aspirant under a spiritual obligation to undergo detachment from the worlds of illusion and conditioning. This brings him to his predestined goal, the domain of reality and absolute liberation.

The searing fire of contrition is the most effective instrument of spiritual progress. In the realm of the spirit, as in the material world, fire is a unique force of transformation and renewal. It must be faced by all who seek salvation. Contrition is a consuming fire for the carnal self, but it is life for the spiritual entity.

♦ Fellowship

It is helpful to the aspirant to have friendly intercourse with more experienced people, for this will enable him to recognize and classify the results achieved at various stages of spiritual development.

(On the path of liberation the function of the spiritual guide is of secondary importance. His task consists in supplying the aspirant with the key to the spiritual treasures concealed within himself, stored within his own nature from eternity. He encourages him by conversing with him from time to time. The spiritual director is like a lighthouse: he is not the goal and he does not carry the aspirant, but simply shows the practicable route to salvation.)

In the way of verification and realization, the master does not invite the pupil. The seeker finds his own guide when he reaches maturity. Since liberation is not available from anyone on request, the aspirant must depend entirely on his own steadfast dedication. The proof of this lies in the fact that even the greatest spiritual masters have been able to lead only a handful of people to annihilation.

♦ Commentary

The way of absolute liberation is for those who are compelled to seek an escape from the torment of relative reality. Some people cannot be content with intellectual and religious attainments. They aspire to the Absolute, to the Essence. These people can find no rest until they attain the Divine Nature, the Quintessence of the Essence. Such is their lofty aspiration.

The Nature of God means the Absolute Ipseity. It is also called by other names, such as the Essence, the Unseen, the Mystery. In all religions, concrete and symbolic representations are provided for the benefit of ordinary people, who are unfamiliar with abstractions. Those who are conscious of the Absolute Ipseity are also conscious of all the relative realities.

The Absolute Ipseity is the source and origin of all religion, theology, and esotericism. It is the capital of the Prophets and Saints. There is no way of reaching it except by annihilation; that is, by discovery and direct experience. It cannot be attained mentally, intellectually, or indirectly. In other words, it can only be reached progressively through the rejection of relativities, the extinction of all that partakes of existence, and the abolition of individualization.

Annihilation is alchemy. Today it saves us from heedlessness, tomorrow it will deliver us from existence. In the words of Mevlânâ, it is the "collyrium of the saints," for it opens the eyes of its owner to the divine mysteries and to realities without end. With the annihilation of actions, all intellectual problems are resolved. With the annihilation of attributes, emotional dependence disappears. With the annihilation of the Essence, all the mystic veils fall away.

On this path of bliss, progress and advancement depend on steadfastness and faithful observance of the practices prescribed. Those who aspire to realization do not strive in vain, for God Himself tells us: "Take one step toward Me and I shall take ten toward you." As closeness increases, the aspirant attains realities the mind could not conceive, beyond his wildest surmise.

As he progresses through the realms of being, the aspirant acquires direct vision of the hidden mysteries. The veils are lifted from his eyes. Occurrences are seen as "non-occurring" and phenomena as "non-events." Opposites combine and mingle.

The Sufism of absolute liberation is normal Sufism. It is the way of the Reality of realities. It is not pantheism or monism. "Existentialist" systems are quite alien to it, for this way is peculiar and exclusive to the "non-existentialists."

The path of verification and realization leads to non-being. It gives access to secrets that may not be divulged.

It does not concern itself with the pursuit of secondary aims, such as beatific vision, reunion, unification, or unity. For those who are predisposed to seek annihilation, the ultimate goal is to achieve non-being, non-existence, the Unseen, and the Absolute Ipseity; in other words, the HUMAN REALITY.

APPENDIX II

Glossary of Sufi Terms

Note: Turkish is the primary language used for the entries in this glossary. Alternate Arabic spellings are indicated with [A] and Persian with [P].

Âb-ı hayât / âb-ı zindegânî [P] (water of life)
The water of life, symbol of immortality, is attained by the traveler on the spiritual path when he achieves liberation (*iṭlāq*) through genuine annihilation (*fanā'*) of the self and is thereby transformed in perpetuity (*baqā'*); by direct experience, he then realizes that life and death are emanations and manifestations of his own essential nature.

The concept of Eternal Life, where self disappears in non-being (*lā-kawn*) and non-individualization (*lā-ta'ayyun*) and where there is neither guide nor goal.

'Abdallāh was a wild and restless type
He went to seek the source of the water of life
By chance he met up with al-Kharaqānī
And there he found the spring of âb-ı zindegânî
He drank his fill
Until
Nor he remained nor Kharaqānī.

KHWĀJA 'ABDALLĀH ANṢĀRĪ

Adem / adem-i ilâhî ('adam / 'adam ilāhī [A]) ([divine] non-existence)
That which is beyond existence.

Synonyms: the secret of existence (*sirr al-wujūd*); the Mystery of mysteries (*ghaib al-ghuyūb*); non-individualization (*lā-ta'ayyun*). According to context, it may also be expressed by such terms as Mystery of the Essence (*ghaib al-dhāt*); secret of identity (*sirr al-huwiyya*); Reality of realities (*ḥaqīqat al-ḥaqā'iq*); absolute quiddity (*māhiyya muṭlaqa*).

In the Noble Qur'ān, this absolute mystery is called the Unseen (*al-ghaib*).

It represents the final stage in the gradual progress through relative "absences" to total extinction. It is the supreme trust, bestowed under the aegis of Muḥammad on those most highly perfected (at the stages of *aḥadiyyet'ül-ayn* and *aḥadiyyet'ül-cem*, qq.v.). This is what the Sufis call direct vision (*'ain*), as opposed to acquired knowledge (*'ilm*).

Adem kibriyâsı (kibriyā' al-'adam [A]) (glory of non-existence)
A term by which the liberated identity expresses its transcendence of all categories of divinity, creation, and being.

It means the total absence and annihilation of all concepts: nature, being, body, and soul, potentiality, and essence—even the concept of divinity. True glory lies in the further extinction of consciousness, perception, and fixity.

It is the human reality (*al-ḥaqīqat al-insāniyya*), also called: the absolute mystery (*al-ghaib al-muṭlaq*); non-individualization (*lāta'ayyun*); loss of separate identity (*ghaib al-huwīya*); the ineffable secret (*al-sirr al-maskūt*).

Adem-i mahz ('adam maḥḍ [A]) (non-existence pure and simple)
For those who take the "existential" view: nothingness (*lā-shay'*). From the "non-existential" viewpoint; that is, according to the view and mystic insight of the Masters of Essential Truth and Reality: the origin and goal, the source and destination of all objectivities.

Seeing that non-existence entails their own destruction, intellect and sensuality are inclined to reject and negate this sublimity of the Divine, which is the supreme beatitude and the ultimate achievement. As for the heart and spirituality, they are ready and eager for this annihilation and total ecstasy, for they recognize that non-existence means eternal salvation and bliss.

Âfak (āfāq [A]) (far horizons)
The external world; that is, the whole system constructed by sensory perception and intellectual comprehension. Antonym: *Enfüs* (*anfus* [A]), the subjective or internal world.

The Qur'ān uses "visible world" (*shahāda*) in contrast with "the Unseen" (*ghaib*). The word "heavens" has the same sense (in the Qur'ānic phrase: "the heavens and the earth" (*al-samāwāti wa-l'arḍ*).

Ahadiyyet (aḥadiyya [A]) (oneness)*

Extinction and non-manifestation. Synonymous with annihilation and non-being. "Non-being" here means genuine or real existence: non-individualization, loss of separate identity, the absolute mystery. The aḥadiyya of physical bodies is the realm of spirits or ideas. This is the level of actions, the aḥadiyya of which is relative non-being. Aḥadiyya of attributes is the realm of absolute non-being.

Ahadiyyet'ül-ayn (aḥadiyyat al-'ain [A]) (oneness of essence)

The extinction of individualization. In the Sufism of Truth and Reality it represents the final stage of development, which they also call "the orphan's property" (*māl al-yatīm*). It is peculiar and exclusive to the venerable Messenger, bearer of the Muḥammadan Reality, or to his heir, in person or by proxy. It can only be received as a gift of grace through direct experience and revelation. In other words, it is a favor bestowed on the "non-existential" Masters. It is the stage of Real Certainty, the station of the Reality of realities. As an idea, it can be understood and handed down, but the direct experience cannot be transmitted to others.

In one sense, it is the exalted mode of being whereby the Lord God transcends even knowledge of Himself.

The term *aḥadiyya muṭlaqa* is synonymous with aḥadiyyat al-'ain.

Ahadiyyet'ül-cem (aḥadiyyat al-jam' [A]) (oneness of integration)

The wholesale annihilation and extinction of the levels of creature and Creator.

Ahadiyyet'ül-kesre (aḥadiyyat al-kathra [A]) (oneness of multiplicity)

The extinction of manifest forms, of individualized multiplicity. It is the level of absolute divinity and essentiality. The primordial individualization, the Maker's awareness of His simple, undifferentiated identity. In this sense, superior to Creativity.

Ahkâm (aḥkām [A]) (rules, laws)

The whole system and regular order of the universe as registered by the mind and senses of one who has not achieved annihilation. The world of obligations, which is the result of the fall from grace.

In the consciousness of one who has achieved annihilation: the world of multiplicity, creation, and particularization, in its stable or permanent aspect "post-integration" (*ba'd al-jam'*).

As perceived by one who has not attained annihilation: the human king-

*In the Sufism of Truth and Reality it does not mean "oneness."

dom, the world, and the cosmos, in their "pre-integration" (*qabl al-jam'*) aspect. (On the return from ecstasy, however, these are seen as the manifest forms of eternal ideas (*a'yan thābita*).

Called the world of particularization (*'ālam al-tafṣīl*), because from this angle (whether spiritual insight has been achieved or is lacking) all laws, names, and attributes give the impression of being actually or potentially observable and present.

Akdesiyyet (aqdasiyya [A]) (holiness in the highest degree)
The state of the level of *ahadiyyet'ül-ayn* (q.v.).

Ultrasanctity. On the path of Truth and Reality, it arises in the movement-from-God (*sair 'ani-llāh*). It is the total absorption of "as if it were not" (*ka-an yam yakun*), which begins with the lightning flash of divine manifestation. When constant and established it represents the Great Intermediacy (*al-barzakhiyyat al-kubrā*) "between the two worlds."

Akl-ı cüzî (al-'aql al-juz'ı [A]) (particular intellect)

Akl-ı kül ('aql al-kull [A]) (universal intellect)
The term "particular intellect" refers to the system of perception based on the five senses; that is, to limited awareness. "Universal intellect" is the term applied to the pure and unrestricted awareness achieved when the senses are transcended through annihilation of the self.

Particular intellect is human knowledge, while universal intellect is divine and essential knowledge. Before annihilation we are in the particular intellect; after annihilation, in the universal intellect. With complete annihilation, annihilation within annihilation, for which the Qur'ānic term is the Ultimate Lotus Tree (*sidrat al-muntahā*), even essential knowledge fades away, yielding to the ultrasanctity of the Unseen. It is because Gabriel symbolizes inspired knowledge (*'ilm ladunnī*) that he cannot pass beyond this boundary point.

Akl-ı kül mazhariyyeti (maẓhariyya 'aql al-kull [A]) (phenomenality of the universal intellect)
Wholeness (synonym: Essence) as opposed to particularization (synonym: attributes).

Dense and concise in its simple purity. In other words, the undifferentiated wholeness of essential knowledge. God's relation to Himself, disregarding His Creativity.

In particular detail: creation's knowledge of His attributes, names, actions, and laws; nature, the fall, humanity.

Arş—Ferş—Kürsi ('arsh—farsh—kursī [A]) (throne—carpet—footstool)
The Throne stands for awareness as the source and recourse of all worlds, manifest and invisible. The inspired comprehension of perfect or most-perfect Masters of the degrees of annihilation. This comprehensive understanding and perfection is alluded to in the proverbial saying: "Hand over hand (everyone has his Master), right up to the Throne," for it is the solution to all problems and the final answer to all questions. Only worldly people have a concrete, physical notion of the Throne.

The Carpet represents superficiality: the external, material, temporal-spatial view of the universe. See *Ahkâm* (*aḥkām*).

The Footstool represents the station, state, and visionary experience of one who has achieved complete annihilation; that is, permanent transformation.

Aşk mecâzî ('ishq majāzī [A]) (metaphorical love)
Aşk hakikî ('ishq ḥaqīqī [A]) (real love)
Metaphorical love is attachment and attraction between persons, or between individuals and God.

Real love is that which overwhelms the traveler on the path of Truth and Reality at the stage of annihilation of the attributes, as a manifestation of the intermediacy (*barzakhiyya*) between necessity and potentiality, between being and non-being.

Aşk-ı mahz ('ishq maḥḍ [A]) (pure love)
As opposed to metaphorical love (see preceding), pure and genuine love is the spiritual intoxication and inebriation arising in the intermediacy of the levels of attributes and Essence.

Love without lover or beloved. In technical language: the ecstasy and mystic inebriation experienced at the borderline of non-existence and being.

The fruit of annihilation, conferred upon the spiritually mature, the Masters of Essence and Reality.

Âyân (a'yān [A]) (objects; substances)
The particulars recognized by perception. These may be graded as follows:

1. Material objects: particular and individual entities noticed by animals and deficient human beings.
2. Natural objects: the things familiar to a normal human being through sensation and knowledge (before he has achieved annihilation). The recognizable objects of the physical world.
3. Objects of knowledge (ideas): these belong to the spiritual world, which lies within the physical world and which manifests itself at the

first step in annihilation; namely, the annihilation of actions or the presence of knowledge. This is the station at which the relative spirit is witnessed.

4. Occult objects: these are proper to the stage of the annihilation of attributes, the degree of relative non-being, where the realms of possibility, intermediacy (*barzakh*), and love are attained. This is the station where existence and non-existence merge. It is also called the degree of prime individualization. Since this means the total cessation of all other individualizations, it carries such names as "non-individualization" and "loss of separate identity."

Âyân-ı mümkûnat (mumkināt [A]) (possibilities, potentialities)
The universe shares the characteristics of existence and non-existence; it is therefore in a state of potentiality. Niyāzī-i Miṣrī was expressing this important truth when he said: "The world has not gone beyond potentiality, take heed!" Compounded of the elements "is" and "is not," the universe hovers between necessity and possibility, both existing and not existing.

Insofar as the universe is seen as the world of potentiality, its particulars and details have been called "possible objects," meaning "manifestations of potentiality."

In terms of the realm of being, we distinguish material objects, physical objects, objects of knowledge, and occult objects. The term "possible objects" applies to these in their entirety.

The unenlightened person sees material and physical (sense) objects. Those devoted to Truth and Reality also witness the objects of knowledge and occult objects: the eternal ideas (*a'yān thābita*).

Âyân-ı sâbite (al-a'yān al-thābita [A]) (stable or permanent objects)
According to the classic definition: "Ideas as realities permanently established in the Knowledge of God."

In their inferior form: ideas accessible to the human mind at the stage of annihilation of actions, when material things and physical bodies, subjectivities and objectivities, are seen as incorporeal forms or abstract images.

On the highest plane: occult ideas, the character and perspective assumed by objects at the level of relative occultation. The permanent abode of the internal and external worlds, lying in reality between being and non-being.

Contemplation of the eternal ideas is contingent on the attainment of annihilation. Failing this, human vision is limited to perceptible objects (*a'yān shahādiyya*); that is, objects accessible to the ordinary senses. For one who has not been blessed with annihilation, such is the "fallen" vision of the universe with its particulars and circumstantialities. From the spiritual point of view, this is the world of separation and lapse from grace.

Ayn ('ain [A]) (eye; essence, substance; self, individuality)
Ordinary meaning: individualization (*ta'ayyun*). Goods, things, creatures, phenomena, objects of concern.

Deeper meaning: the ultrasanctity of the Unseen, which is the opposite and also the underlying reality of the visible universe.

The four or five orders of being are usually summed up in two; namely, *'ain* and *'ilm* (knowledge), representing the range of vision of the accomplished spiritual traveller. The terms *'ain* and *'ilm* correspond to the Qur'ānic *ghaib* (the Unseen) and *shahāda* (the visible world) respectively.

Ayn-el yakin ('ain al-yaqīn [A]) (eye of certainty)
Mastery of the innermost realities, the divine mysteries, is on three basic levels:

Knowledge of Certainty (*'ilm al-yaqīn*)
Vision of Certainty (*'ain al-yaqīn*)
Truth of Certainty (*ḥaqq al-yaqīn*)

Knowledge of Certainty is the intimacy achieved by the seeker at the stage of annihilation of actions, through attaining the presence of knowledge. From that moment on, the individual's knowledge is precisely the Knowledge of Essence.

Vision of Certainty is the view of the universe as it impresses itself on the seeker of Truth and Reality at the stage of annihilation of attributes. The states of intermediacy (*barzakhiyya*) and Love become manifest.

Truth of Certainty is the extinction and non-existence brought about in the intimacy of the annihilation of personal individuality.

Ayniyyet-i Muhammadiyye (al-'ainiyyat al-Muḥammadiyya [A]) (the Muḥammadan Identity)
The degree of holiness and ultrasanctity acquired, after the annihilation of actions, by one on the path of Truth and Reality who possesses the aptitude for the extinction of individuality. If real and mystically bestowed annihilation manifests itself in any spiritual traveler, he is deemed to be endowed with the Muḥammadan Identity.

It embraces the legislative, informative, and missionary aspects of Prophethood and symbolizes, above all, the spiritual offices of deputy, shaikh, teacher, cardinal, saint, and Helper of the Age.

The highest level of development and the most comprehensive consciousness predestined for mankind. A spiritual mantle, mystically inherited in unbroken succession. The world is never devoid of an individual holding this "Supreme Trust."

Aynûnet ('ainūna [A]) (abstract vision)
The state of the degree of mystic vision (*'ain*). Opposite of being/becoming (*kainūna*). Essence without attributes.

Baka (baqā' [A]) (permanence, survival, subsistence)
Annihilation within annihilation: finding consummation and a permanent abode in the ultrasanctity of non-existence.

Essence-manifestation occurs in the seeker of Truth and Reality on completion of the stages of annihilation (*fanā'*). This state is therefore called the end of annihilation.

The movement-from-God occurs in survival beyond annihilation. The beatitude of "as if it were not" is conferred at this station.

Bâtın (bāṭin [A]) (inner, inward, internal; hidden, secret)
The divine mysteries (*ladunniyyāt*) attained through annihilation in God (*fanā' fī-llāh*). That which underlies every level and every realm in the entire universe. The inner aspect of the material level is the domain of sense perception. The realm of knowledge is the inner aspect of the organic level. The inner aspect of the realm of knowledge is the station of relative occultation; that is, the annihilation of attributes. As for the realm of absolute occultation (*ghaib muṭlaq*), this is the absolute innermost of all other levels and realms.

Berzahiyyet (barzakhiyya [A]) (intermediate state)
Berzahiyyet-i kiibra (al-barzakhiyyat al-kubra [A]) (greatest intermediacy)
The interval between the two realms of being; comparable to dawn or dusk as intermediate stages between night and day.

The Greatest Intermediacy is the supreme interval: the mediating and interpreting role of comprehensive perception; that is, of the perfect man, between the visible and Unseen worlds.

Beşer (al-bashar [A]) (mankind)
Âdem (Ādam [A]) (Adam)
The image or extension of perception.

Consciousness intermediate between the base material realm (that is, the inanimate, animal, and anthropoid levels) and the realm of knowledge; the normal human condition of complete involvement in the external, physical world of sense perception. Other terms include the lower world (*dunyā*); potentialities (*mumkināt*); humanity (*nāsūt*).

Bivücûdî (bī-vujūdi [P]) (non-being)
Bihôdi (bī-khōdī [P]) (ecstasy)
The state peculiar to the true human realm: the "as if it were not" achieved at the end of their spiritual journey by seekers devoted to Reality and Essence. The blissful taste of the final station.

Other Sufi terms for this include extinction (*istihlāk*); rapturous absorption (*istighrāq*); lover's union (*wiṣāl*); beauty (*jamāl*); mystery (*ghaib*).

Câmiiyyet (jāmi'iyya [A]) (comprehensiveness)
Câmiiyyet-i gaybiyye (ghaibiyya [A]) (mystic comprehensiveness)
Câmiiyyet-i ilâhiyye (jāmi'iyya ilāhiyya [A]) (divine comprehensiveness)
Câmiiyyet-i sifâtiyye ve esmâiyye (ṣifātiyya wa-asmā'iyya [A]) (comprehensiveness of attributes and names)
Comprehensiveness is the power of perception to embrace the levels of divine Truth and creation (as a result of the fact that the externally manifest consists of the particulars of perception and knowledge).

In the saying "There is nothing in the universe except the Perfect Man," the term "Perfect Man" (*insān kāmil*) is a symbolic personification of the abstract concept "perception" (*idrāk*). Man consists of perception. In his ordinary humanity he is limited perception, whereas his real nature is pure perception, comprehensive perception, which comprises the higher and the lower, the individualizations of the hidden and of the manifest.

"Divine comprehensiveness" is a polite term for the universal comprehension of man; that is, of perception. This comprehension includes the power to comprehend attributes, names, actions, and laws (in other words, the realms of the relative occult, knowledge, the organic, and the material).

"Mystic comprehensiveness"—the human reality—is the modality whereby all degrees of being are secreted in the Absolute Unseen and gradually descend therefrom.

Cemâl (jamāl [A]) (beauty, esp. the divine beauty)
The opposite of *jalāl* (Majesty). Synonymous in Sufism with the divine Compassion (as in the formula "In the name of God, All-Merciful and Compassionate"). It is as the All-Merciful—in His aspect of Majesty—that the Lord God brings forth creation, whereas it is as the Compassionate—in

His aspect of Beauty—that He bestows upon the universe the bounties of mystery, inwardness, and non-existence.

It is absurd to take the concept of Beauty in a literal or figurative sense. On the path of Truth and Reality, no attention is paid to the superficial interpretation of Qur'ānic verses or Prophetic sayings, nor to the symbolism of traditional Sufism; it is rather their inner meanings that are received, as the result of mystic revelation.

Cezbe (jadhba [A]) (attraction; ecstasy, rapture)
The effect of annihilation (*fanā'*).

The state of the seeker of Truth and Reality who has passed from limited perception to absolute perception. This state becomes permanent as one makes progress along the spiritual path.

Genuine rapture is that gradual extinction and absorption by which the seeker rises to higher levels of perception. It is increase in the penetration of vision and attainment of the hidden worlds.

Pathological states are not accepted as rapture in the Sufism of Truth and Reality.

Cismiyyet / cismâniyyet (jismiyya / jusmāniyya [A]) (physicality)
The concrete individualizations of the inanimate, material, physical, and sensory levels, which lie below the level of eternal ideas. To unenlightened eyes: the impression made by external forms. This narrow view can be transcended only through annihilation, starting from the realm of knowledge.

As seen by one who has not yet come to annihilation, potential objects assume physical solidity. When annihilation is achieved, they are transformed into objects of knowledge or occult objects: this is the world of eternal ideas (*a'yān thābita*).

Dâim-ül ebedî (al-dā'im al-abadī [A]) (the eternally enduring)
An expression used by the venerable Muḥyī-l Dīn ibn al-'Arabī, the Greatest Shaikh, in his description of Adam: "New from all eternity, eternally enduring youth." This is a way of saying that—since in reality man consists of perception—the human essence is everlasting, from all eternity to all eternity.

According to the Masters of Truth and Reality, the nature of Adam (that is, of perception) is even more exalted than this, since the very concepts of past and future eternity are mere fragments of perception, derivatives of consciousness.

Dîniyyât (dîniyyāt [A]) (religious doctrines)
Theology. Condescensions of absolute truth.

Rules and instructions designed to ensure human felicity in this world and in the hereafter.

There are primitive (non-divine) religions; religions based on divine scriptures and Prophetic missions; religious teachings which have as their basis the pursuit of Truth and Reality.

Ef'âl (af'āl [A]) (actions, deeds)
Visions of the spiritual universe: objects of knowledge as they appear, through the blessed gift of annihilation, to the seeker of Truth and Reality who enters the realm of knowledge. The states experienced as the result of this vision.

The inebriation of knowledge is experienced at this stage.

Enfüs (anfus [A]) (souls)
In the Sufism of Truth and Reality: the worlds of the Unseen; mystic revelations. These are the absolute and essential meanings of the term. The Qur'ānic verse "To God belongs the mystery of the heavens and the earth" is understood by the seeker of Truth and Reality as meaning "God is the extinction of the outer [*āfaq*] and the inner universe [*anfus*]."

Ervâh (arwāh [A]) (spirits)
The concept "spirit" (*rūḥ*) is graded according to whether it is incarnate, relative, or absolute. Its manifestation at the annihilation of actions, that is, in the realm of knowledge, is relative spirit.

The incorporeal particulars of the created universe, which become visible to the seeker of Truth and Reality at the first station on the way of voluntary death.

Ervâh âlemi ('ālam al-arwāḥ [A]) (world of spirits)
The vista of the first secret level, which opens to the seeker's eye with the granting of the vision of ideas; that is, with the experience of annihilation of actions.

Terms like "spirit(s)" or "soul(s)" are unscientific expressions taken from the sacred scriptures. The technical term is "objects of knowledge" (*a'yān 'ilmiyya*), the first step toward the eternal ideas (*a'yān thābita*).

Esmâ (asmā' [A]) (names)
Particulars of the detailed self-knowledge of the Essence in the realm of relative occultation. Synonymous with *ṣifāt* (attributes).

Fasıl—vasıl (faṣl—waṣl [A]) (separation—conjunction)
In High Sufism,* "separation" is knowledge (*'ilm*), while "conjunction" is direct vision (*'ain*). These two constitute the summation of the realms of being. This summation is peculiar to the special path, in contrast to the common path with its four or five realms.

The terms "integration and particularization" (jam' wa-taflṣīl) are also used.

If you have understood the symbolism of integration and
particularization, hold your peace.
There's nothing more to talk about thereafter with
servants or with kings.

NIYĀZĪ-I MIṢRĪ

Fenâ (fanā' [A]) (annihilation, extinction)
Annihilation is becoming non-existent; passing from the manifest to the unmanifest, from the relative to the absolute, from stability to extinction. Its consummation is perpetuity (*baqā›*) in non-existence.

Liberation (*iṭlāq*) is the harmonizing, blending, and mutual annihilating of opposites, which can never come about unless our perception achieves the alchemy of annihilation.

Liberation begins with annihilation and reaches its consummation in perpetuity.

Liberation is symbolized in our world by dawn and sunset, for night and day become one at daybreak and nightfall. This explains the important Sufi concept of "integration-with-differentiation" (*al-jam'ma'a-lfarq*). Here we have the key to the Qur'ānic riddle "Lord of the two Easts (risings) and Lord of the two Wests (settings)."

The Lord of these temporal events is symbolic of perception as the origin and end of necessity and potentiality.

Stages of annihilation:

These stages are mystically conferred degrees of progress from potentiality to necessity; that is, from being to non-being. They can be achieved only on the path of Truth and Reality. They are experienced in actual reality, not notionally, mentally, or by transference.

---

*Editor's note: According to Nevit Ergin, High Sufism refers to the path to reach Fenâ. Before Fenâ, everything is knowledge, literatures, theories, talk, separation. After Fenâ, there is no knowledge, no king, no servant, only Essence.

These ascending levels of perception are:

Annihilation of laws (fanā' al-aḥkām). The condition of a normal human being, who has passed from the world of matter to that of sense perception; that is, the organic world. This is not considered a genuine annihilation.

Annihilation of actions (fanā' al-af'āl). Upward progress from the realm of sense perception to the realm of knowledge (that is, the spiritual world) and the achievement of ideation. The most difficult stage to attain, it marks the beginning of the eternal ideas.

Annihilation of attributes (fanā' al-ṣifāt). Ascension to the realm of relative occultation, where the aspirant experiences the inebriation of real love on beholding the eternal ideas. The station of potentiality and intermediacy, it is the extremity of the eternal ideas.

Annihilation of the Essence (fanā' al-dhāt). Also called the absolute annihilation, the divine occultation, the mystery of being, and so on. The stage of consummation for the abolition of individualization and the extinction of properties of being.

Other terms for this ultimate stage are "complete annihilation" and "annihilation within annihilation." It is the point at which annihilation acquires permanence (*baqā'*).

Fenâ fillâh (fanā' fī-llāh [A]) (annihilation in God)
Fenâ fir'Resûl (fanā' fī-lrasūl [A]) (annihilation in the Messenger)
Fenâ fiş'şeyh (fanā' fī-lshaikh [A]) (annihilation in the Shaikh)
Concepts peculiar to monistic Sufism, with its theory of the unicity of Being. With the exception of annihilation in God, they have no validity in the eyes of those who ascend from the stage of practical wisdom to the level of Reality; that is, those who progress to liberation by the path of Truth and Reality.

Annihilation in God is the extinction of potentiality in necessity, the immersion of being in non-being. It is the attainment of non-existence; which is genuine being, through mystic attraction away from relative, material existence. The achievement of positive non-existence, that is, the universal source, the origin and destination of all beings, perceptibles, and intelligibles. In abbreviated form, simply "annihilation."

Ferdiyyet (fardiyya [A]) (singularity; individuality)
The incorporeality and transcendence of the Essence in relation to its own particularization. In Sufism, the peculiar station of the Cardinal Saint (*quṭb*), permanently established in complete annihilation and non-existence.

In his work entitled *Fuṣūṣ al-ḥikam,* the venerable Ibn al-'Arabī uses the expression "Singular Wisdom" (*ḥikma fardiyya*) in reference to the noble Messenger.

Feyz'i akdes (al-faiḍ al-aqdas [A]) (most holy emanation)
The capability of the absolute Essence to know itself as an undifferentiated whole.

God's awareness of His Essence, devoid of attributes, names, actions, and laws.

Feyz'i mukaddes (al-faiḍ al-muqaddas [A]) (sanctified emanation)
The capability of the divine Truth to know itself in particular detail. Laws, actions, names, and attributes become manifest and established through this emanation. Also called the Creative Power.

Gavs (ghawth [A]) (succor, deliverance)
The Cardinal of cardinals (*quṭb al-aqṭāb*), who combines the cardinality of spiritual guidance with that of Being.

Whether in the worldly or mystic sphere, the title signifies a person who is a source of grace and blessings: one to whom people turn for succour and help.

In Sufism, the most competent and highly advanced personality of the age. Some maintain that the phenomena of the universe revolve around this person's spirit. He is considered to be the heir of the Prophet Muḥammad.

Gayb (ghaib [A]) (absence; invisibility; occultation)
The unmanifest.

In the absolute sense, the innermost and highest degree of extinction for each being and concept; for example, for inanimate matter ghaib is the organic realm, for which in turn ghaib is the realm of knowledge. Relative occultation is ghaib for the realm of knowledge or spirit. All realms have their ghaib in the absolute occultation, which is also known as the divine Unseen, the mystery of the Essence, loss of separate identity, the quintessence of the Essence, pure mystery, Mystery of mysteries, and so on.

Nothing can lie beyond the absolute ghaib, which is the ultimate secret of existence: the liberated soul and divine non-existence.

Hak (ḥaqq [A]) (truth; the divine truth)
Hakkiyyet (ḥaqqiyya [A]) (truth-as-divinity)
Origin and destination of the created universe. Allāh, the divine Person or Essence, the Lord, the One to Whom all worship is due. The unmanifest element in the dualistic system produced by our particular perception with its

need to differentiate and distinguish. The manifest element is the created world, otherwise known as the lower world, potentiality, humanity, and so on. The contrast is also expressed as *God—everything else.*

The principle of Truth-as-Divinity, properly understood, is the concept of Creativity and Effective Godhead. Absolute Truth is the Mysterious Unitary Divinity. In this it transcends creation.

Hakâik (ḥaqā'iq [A]) (realities)
Hidden quiddities, secrets, mysteries, which are accessible only through annihilation (*fanā'*). Opposite of rituals, formalities, externals.

Externals are for heedless people; realities are the peculiar property of those who master annihilation and perpetual non-being. As the Prophetic Tradition puts it: "Ordinary people are asleep and only wake up when they die."

However, ritual and formal acts of worship are not abandoned by those who have attained the realities, even though they have transcended such obligations. They are always inwardly in touch with reality, even while performing duties belonging to laws and potentiality.

Hâl (ḥāl [A]) (state, condition)
Kaal (qāl [A]) (saying, speech)
In Sufism *qāl* refers to knowledge acquired mentally and by transmission. On annihilation this gives way to *ḥāl,* as it moves from the outer to the inner and takes on an experiential and mystically revealed character.

Qāl is allotted to those on the exoteric path and to monistic mystics.

Ḥāl is the fruit of the stations of permanent non-being and liberation, the degrees of realization achieved through progressive annihilation and rapture by genuine Sufis, those who aspire to Essence and Reality. The latter are very rare.

Halkiyyet (khalqiyya [A]) (createdness)
The total system of the universe of being and becoming, as it impresses itself on those who have not achieved annihilation. Opposite of *ḥaqqiyya.*

Khalqiyya is relative. From the viewpoint of Truth and Reality it is the capability of the Essence to know itself in detail through revelation from above. To the unenlightened this appears as the universe.

Hazret (ḥaḍra [A]) (presence)
Hazerât (ḥaḍarāt [A]) (presences)
The stages of attendance, vicinity, proximity, nearness, contiguity, and arrival.

In Sufism spiritual progress proceeds through the "presences" of being. Five presences are generally recognized: the realms of matter, sense perception, knowledge, relative mystery, and absolute mystery. Certain authors omit the realm of matter, mentioning as a presence the realm of symbols, which they place between sense perception and knowledge. This is the system of dreams and waking intuitions.

Many other terms are applied to each of these stages. Terms used for the presence of knowledge, for instance, include: the world of souls or spirits (*arwāḥ*); the world of power (*jabarūt*); the sanctified emanation; the second individualization; annihilation of actions; and so on.

The presence of absolute mystery is likewise known by many names, such as annihilation of the Essence; non-individualization; the secret; non-being; the absolute emanation; extinction of individualization; extinction of integration.

The presences, that is, the stages of annihilation, are accessible exclusively by direct experience and mystic revelation on the path of Truth and Reality. They are reached by gradual progress in deeper and deeper self-discipline. It takes ten to fifteen years of spiritual exercises, invocations, and contrition to attain each presence. Though difficult, it is not impossible.

The presences are summed up as insight (*'ain*) and knowledge (*'ilm*), corresponding respectively to the Unseen and visible worlds.

Heyâkil (hayākil [A]) (statues; temples; bodily forms)
Images.

The corporeal—imaginary—aspect of the eternal ideas, viewed only as manifest forms. Also called phantoms.

> *Our souls are our phantoms,*
> *Our phantoms are our souls.*
>
> JUNAID AL-BAGHDĀDĪ

Heyemân (hayamān [A]) (love's rapture)
The bewilderment of love.

On the path of Truth and Reality, the semi-absorption of the aspirant, midway between the external world and the realm of the divine Ipseity. A state between being and non-being, that is, between potentiality and necessity, induced in those constantly inebriated with real love.

The extinction of affectionate love. It is manifest in its complete perfection only in relative occultation, on the annihilation of attributes.

Heyûlâ (hayūlā [A from Gk.]) (matter)
The vague and defective perception of things or phenomena in incompletely manifest form.

There is base matter and noble matter.

Base matter (primary matter) is the impression of the world registered by minerals, plants, animals, and humans of incomplete perception. It is the lowest level of being, inferior to the realm of sense perception; that is, the complete manifestation perceived by humans with normal faculties.

Noble matter (secondary matter) is the "black light" or "blindness," which rests on the threshold of the Unseen, between the annihilation of attributes and the annihilation of Essence. Beyond it lies the heavenly ascension (*mi'rāj*); that is, the "lightning flash of Essential manifestation."

Hilâfet (khilāfa [A]) (vicarship; succession)
Genuine vicarship is the station of one who has reached annihilation on the path of Truth and Reality. Right guidance is its important corollary.

On reaching even the first stage of annihilation, the annihilation of actions, the aspirant acquires divine bounties and Muḥammadan capacities, for he gains access by experience and mystic revelation to the essential realities and esoteric knowledge.

This stage is also called the rank of cardinal (*quṭbiyya*) or of Universal Helper (*ghawthiyya*). One who inherits this station is known as the Master of the Age.

Hilkat (khilqa [A]) (creation; nature)
The capability of the Supreme Truth to know itself in detail. The phenomenal universe of limited human perception.

Also called the world of being, of beings, of things brought into being, of potential beings, of the fall, of humanity, and so on.

A non-event from the point of view of one who has "arrived."

> *The world has not passed beyond potentiality; do not fail*
> *to take heed.*
>
> NIYĀZĪ-I MIṢRĪ

His-şahâdet hazreti (ḥaḍrat al-ḥiss wa-lshahāda [A]) (presence of sense-perception)
The organic world. The universe as perceived by the ordinary human being; that is, one who has not attained annihilation. The presence of being superior to that of matter. Above and within this lies the presence of knowledge, also known as the spiritual world.

Hû (Hū [A]) (He)
Hüviyyet (huwiyya [A]) (identity; Ipseity)
The vocable *Hū* denotes the ultimate degree; namely, the Divine or Essential Reality, while *huwiyya* is a term for this station.

According to the venerable Najm al-Dīn al-Kubrā, "The letter 'h' in the divine name Allāh is the sound we make with every breath. The other letters (in the Arabic spelling) represent an intensified definite article. The essential part of the divine name is therefore that 'h,' which automatically accompanies every breath we take. All life depends on the constant utterance of that noble name."

The same meaning is conveyed by such terms as "absolute Ipseity," "pure Ipseity," and "the secret of Being." In the eyes of those who regard non-being as the highest goal, it represents the supreme holiness of non-existence.

İcmâl (ijmāl [A]) (summation)

Opposite of particularization or detailing (*tafṣīl*).

Pure perception of the realities, whereby the degrees of creation and divine Truth are observed as an integral whole. The condition of the perfect man; that is, the first individualization.

An aspect of liberation (*iṭlāq*), where all summations and particularizations merge.

ifnâ'i Vücûdiyyât (ifnā' al-wujūdiyyāt [A]) (destruction of the properties of being)

The gradual disappearance of the impression of the world, of the sense of existence, to be replaced first by potentiality and finally by non-existence. This occurs in proportion to the aspirant's progress through the stages of annihilation.

İlhâm (ilhām [A]) (inspiration)

Revelations from the heart to the mind.

Communications from God to His servants.

If these do not have the character of mental association of ideas, they are considered to be various forms of genuine inspiration; otherwise they are illusions or ordinary thoughts.

Related terms are *waḥy* (inspiration, revelation); *khiṭāb* (message); *hātif* (mysterious voice).

Such inspiration occurs in the traveler on the path of Truth and Reality before he reaches annihilation, in the phase of movement-toward-God (*sair ilā-Ilāh*). As in the case of prophetic inspiration, which also begins in a similar fashion, it becomes progressively steadier and stronger.

It also occurs at the stages of annihilation.

İlm ('ilm [A]) (knowledge)

The Ipseity's capability of condescensions to its own Essentiality, Divinity, and Creativity. This potential consciousness is externally manifest as the creation.

The degrees of Truth and creation are, in reality, contingencies of knowledge, gradations of perception, levels of awareness.

On those who have not achieved annihilation, knowledge leaves the impression of a universe of beings, bodies, affairs, and phenomena. Deliverance from this impression begins with the annihilation of actions, which is called the presence of knowledge. The most primitive part of knowledge is the level of matter (*hayūlā*). Knowledge disappears in the Absolute Mystery, giving way to insight (*'ain*).

The boundary between knowledge and mystery is referred to in the Qur'ān as the Ultimate Lotus Tree, beyond which Gabriel cannot pass.

İmkân—Vucûb (imkān—wujūb [A]) (possibility—necessity)
The potentiality of self-knowledge on the part of the Supreme Truth, both in summary and in detail, is the universe, the manifest and unmanifest, the degrees of creation and Truth. The created universe is called the world of potentiality.

"Necessity" is that whereby the Essence of Truth transcends and is immune from this knowledge and contingency.

According to the Masters of Reality, necessity is the Unseen and non-existence, while potentiality is the universe: external, internal; perceptible, intelligible.

The descent to potentiality is through the "Reality of Adam"; the return to necessity is by the guidance of the "Reality of Muḥammad."

İnsilâh (insilākh [A]) (stripping away)
İstiğrak (istighrāq [A]) (immersion)
Insilākh is a contact occurring between our outer and our inner, that is, between our sensuality and our spirituality (our subconscious), whether in sleep or in a waking state. True dreams come into this category, as do visions experienced either in a waking state or between sleep and wakefulness.

"Immersion" is ecstasy, separation from the body. In the novice it occurs only spasmodically and briefly, becoming gradually more prolonged in the advanced aspirant. Also called *istihlāk* (being consumed), *wajd* (ecstasy), and *jadhba* (rapture). "Essential manifestation" is this too.

İrâdî ölüm [T] (irādī [A]) (voluntary death)
Tahkik Oliimii [T] (taḥqīq [A]) (death of realization)
The states of rapture, ecstasy, and passing into non-existence, which occur in the traveler on the path of Truth and Reality as he progresses through mystic revelation in the stages of annihilation. Consummation comes with complete annihilation; that is, non-existence in perpetuity (*baqā'*).

This is the ultraholiness of the "perfect poverty" referred to in the Prophetic Tradition: "When poverty is complete, there is Allāh."

Known and understood theoretically at the levels of sacred law, mystical systems, and practical wisdom; but its realization depends on the quest for liberation, experience of annihilation and rapture, and arrival at the stage of Reality. It is granted exclusively to the great saints, the Masters of Essence, Reality, and Non-Existence.

İşâret (ishāra [A]) (sign)
Âlâmet ('alāma [A]) (sign)
Premonitory indications, observed in connection with the explanation and interpretation of cosmic phenomena. Prediction of human destinies, subjective or objective, from things and events. On the path of Truth and Reality, this area starts in the vicinity of annihilation.

Such "signs" are intimations of the states of prophecy.

Dreams almost always stem from physical, organic influences and are therefore invalid and deceptive, whereas signs are always quickly proved correct. This is corroborated by the Noble Qur'ān.

İysâr'ı vücûd (īthār al-wujūd [A]) (bestowal of being)
The divine condescension, through the most holy emanation, from absolute mystery to the first individualization. God's attachment to His Essence is the first stage in the bestowal of Being: the Truth's knowledge of Itself as an integral whole.

In detail also, with God's condescension to His attributes, actions, and laws, the bestowal of Being is in comprehensiveness and perfection. These are not temporal but primordial, essential.

Kâlb (qalb [A]) (heart)
Kâlb'ı selim (qalb salīm [A]) (sound heart)
The heart (*QaLB*) represents the attainment of annihilation, for it possesses the character of transformation (*taQLīB*) between potentiality and necessity. To be master of the heart means to be master of annihilation. The "sound heart" is the condition of direct vision proper to the masters of permanent non-existence, who are at the stage of complete annihilation. It has other names, such as the Great Intermediacy, the Muḥammadan Vicarship, the Cardinality of Guidance and Being, and so on. In theoretical Sufism it is called "the Divine Subtlety." In one sense heart is also the "comprehensive human reality."

Kevn'i câmi' (al-kawn al-jāmi' [A]) (the comprehensive cosmos)
The human being.

The Greater World, that is, perception, is the "lesser transcript," while the human reality, which is the totality of necessity and potentiality, is the "greater transcript." It is called the comprehensive cosmos. It embraces the degrees of Truth and creation and is the bearer of the divine mantle.

"The lines below and the letters above," that is, the universe of individualizations, arise, become established, and disappear in non-existence, in the non-being that is the human reality.

Keynûnet (kainūna [A]) (being, becoming)
As regards stability, this is the densest degree of perception, the gradations of which are occultation, visuality, and being. Also known by such names as cosmic existence, the world of material phenomena, the lower world, humanity, and so on.

Bodily forms, that is, things, appear at this level; images of light become apparent at the level of visuality; at the level of occultation, the glory of "as if it were not" is reached.

Kurb'u nevâfil (qurb al-nawāfil [A]) (intimacy of supererogatory worship)
Kurb'u ferâiz (qurb al-farā'iḍ [A]) (intimacy of obligatory worship)
Kurb'u mutlak (qurb muṭlaq [A]) (absolute intimacy)
On the path of liberation, from the viewpoint of Truth and Reality, cosmic substances are seen as the intimacy of supererogatory worship. The permanent substances (eternal ideas) are viewed as the intimacy of obligatory worship. As for absolute intimacy, this is the state of intermediacy, between the annihilation of attributes and the annihilation of essence. It is the threshold of the extinction of individuality. Other interpretations of the degrees of intimacy are only theoretical.

Ceberût (jabarūt [A]) (the world of power)
Lâhût (lāhūt [A]) (divinity)
Melekût (malakūt [A]) (the world of sovereignty)
The lower world is "humanity," the world of property. The spiritual world is the "world of power," the stage of intensity and purification. Contemplation of the occult substances is the "world of sovereignty." The world of the Essence is "divinity." These are equivalent to the "presences of Being."
Nâsût (nāsūt [A]) (humanity)

Mârifet (ma'rifa [A]) (intuitive knowledge; gnosis)
The gradations of Sufism are mentioned in the Prophetic Tradition:

My words: the *sharī'a* (sacred law)

My conduct: the *ṭarīqa* (mystical path)

My ready cash: *ma'rifa* (gnostic wisdom)

My capital: *ḥaqīqa* (reality)

The phase of *ma'rifa* corresponds to the unitary and monistic outlook that lies between imitation and verification.

As seen without the achievement of realization, it represents the level of theoretical and mental certainty. But in the eyes of the Masters of Reality this is a stage that must be surpassed, for it is one of consolation (*tasallī*), not of manifestation (*tajallī*).

Muâyenât'ı basariyye (mu'āyanāt baṣariyya [A]) (optical observations)
Müşâhedâ'ı gaybiyye (mushāhadāt ghaibiyya [A]) (occult visions)
The manner in which, at the stages of annihilation, cosmic substances appear as eternal ideas (*a'yān thābita*). This is observed by both the eye of the head and the eye of the heart: under the auspices of essential knowledge, in the presence of knowledge, and in the presence of relative occultation.

Among the blessings of annihilation and the marvels of realization. Attained only through strict contrition and spiritual exercises, practiced over a long period of time.

Mukakkik (muḥaqqiq [A]) (one who seeks truth and reality)
The Master of Truth and Reality, who has steadily progressed in liberation to achieve permanent transformation by traveling the path of rapture, annihilation, ecstasy, and realization. The genuine Sufi Master, who is at the level of the Reality of realities.

Apart from the Messengers, only the great saints and "Essentialists" belong in this category. When he attains perfection, the Master of Truth and Reality is endowed with the Muḥammadan heritage; that is, the role of Universal Pivot and Helper.

Mutlak (muṭlaq [A]) (absolute)
Opposite of relative.

Non-existence. Non-being.

Non-awareness.

Absence. Positive non-existence.

Absolute Being means existence transcending being; that is, non-being, the Unseen, the mystery of Being.

Its attainment is dependent on a capacity for extinction of the individuality, possible through prolonged striving and contrition on the path of annihilation.

Nefes'i Rahmânî (nafas raḥmānī [A]) (breath of divine mercy)
A name for the "sanctified emanation."

The cause of the emergence of creation is God's All-Mercifulness, which is known in Sufism as the "breath of divine mercy." An expression surviving from the Middle Ages, like nearly all Sufi expressions.

Nûr (nūr [A]) (light)
Nûr'u siyâh [P] (black light)
The "Supreme Blackness." At its lowest, what is manifest in the universe. At its highest, what is concealed in the annihilations.

Its inner aspect is "mystery" or "secret."

The venerable Jalāl al-Dīn Rūmī said: "We are endowed with the illuminations of the Messenger, but Shams-i Tabrīz is endowed with his secrets."

Black light is the luminosity of the intermediacy linking the degrees of annihilation with permanent non-being, the radiance of the Integration of integration. This is symbolized by the black garments worn by the Masters of Annihilation and by religious men in imitation of these.

The "Supreme Blackness" is the same concept.

Nüzûl (nuzūl [A]) (descent)
Urûc ('urūj [A]) (ascent)
"Descent" refers to the descending scale from Divinity (*lāhūt*) to humanity (*nāsūt*). This descent is from Truth to creation.

"Ascent" refers to the ascending or rising scale, from humanity to Divinity (lāhūt). This ascent is from creation to Truth.

Describing the Way of the Malāmiyya-Nūriyya, 'Abd al-Raḥīm Fadā'ī (Fedâ'î Efendi), deputy of the venerable Nūr al-'Arabī, said: "Our lower path is the ascent from creation to Truth; our higher path is the descent from Truth to creation."

Rûh (rūḥ [A]) (soul; spirit)
Rûh hazreti (ḥaḍrat al-rūḥ [A]) (presence of the soul or spirit)
There is the animal spirit, the relative spirit, and the absolute spirit.

The presence of the spirit is the level of the relative spirit; that is, the view of the objects of knowledge that presents itself to those who pursue Reality, in the presence of knowledge, upon the annihilation of actions.

The animal spirit is physical life, incarnate in the body.

The absolute spirit is the Absolute Mystery, which is the source, origin, and destination of all individualizations, the self-subsisting cause of their being.

Another term is the Supreme Spirit, which is a title given to the Universal

Helper. Royal Spirit refers to the aptitude for annihilation and permanent non-being, proper to those who contemplate the hereafter.

The Holy Spirit is the essential knowledge that comes with annihilation.

Seyr'i sülûk (sayr al-sulūk [A]) (traversing the path)
Sâlik (sālik [A]) (wayfarer)
Traversing the path may be theoretical or real.

In imitative and monistic Sufism it remains theoretical, always retaining a mental, intellectual, and traditional character. The stages and stations are passed over without direct mystical experience, in sessions devoted to marvelous tales, the interpretation of dreams, and friendly discussion of such themes.

This does not satisfy seekers with high aspirations. Having come to the right degree of inward maturity, they make contact with a perfect teacher capable of perfecting others. They then embark on the real journey to annihilation, which is development toward liberation and the quest of Truth and Reality.

The "seeker" (*ṭālib*) in the theoretical sphere now becomes a "wayfarer" (*sālik*).

Genuine progress on the path is dependent on real mystic experience of the presences of being; that is, the degrees of annihilation. The vehicles and rules of this road are dhikr of the breath, spiritual exercises, contrition, and friendly intercourse. The way is hard and long, but it guarantees manifestations and union, maybe even freedom from the need for union. This is in contrast to the consolation and anticipation of the theoretical path.

Sıfât (ṣifāt [A]) (qualities; attributes)
Manifestations in the interval between insight (*'ain*) and knowledge (*'ilm*).

Particulars within the Essential consciousness, above laws and actions. Also called "names" (*asmā'*).

Divinity (*ṣamadāniyya*) and Oneness (*aḥadiyya*) are the absolute attributes.

The essential attributes are Being (*wujūd*), Permanence (*baqā'*), Primordiality (*qidam*), Uniqueness (*waḥdāniyya*), Incomparability (*mukhālafatun lil-ḥawādith*), Self-subsistence (*qiyām bi-nafsihi*).

The positive attributes are Life, Power, Knowledge, Will, Hearing, Sight, Speech, and Creation.

The absolute attributes are relative to the Divine Mystery, the essential attributes to Singleness, the positive attributes to humanity. Another category is that of the effective attributes; that is, the particularization of Power (*qudra*).

Suver'i ilmiyye (ṣuwar 'ilmiyya [A]) (knowable forms; ideas)
To us in our ordinary human condition, things and phenomena appear materially substantial.

In the eyes of one who "awakes from humanity" by achieving annihilation, these corporealities are transformed into "cognizables." The particulars of the universe, that is, things and phenomena, come to be perceived as "knowable forms."

As progress is made in annihilation, this mode of seeing becomes established and the world of eternal ideas (*a'yān thābita*) becomes visible. This is the stage of sanctity (*qudsiyya*).

The venerable Khwāja 'Ubaidallāh al-Aḥrār said: "Absolute Being becomes manifest through its own knowable forms."

Knowable forms are among the divine revelations.

Tahkik (taḥqīq [A]) (verification, realization)
Taḥqiq is the Sufism of annihilation and permanent non-being (*fanā'—baqā'*). It is the esoteric path with liberation as its goal. Mental, intellectual, and traditional connections with Sufism are "imitation" (*taqlīd*). The genuine Sufism is the quest for Truth and Reality, which presupposes mystical revelation and transformational experience.

There is no way to achieve this except by voluntary death. We have corroboration and confirmation of this in Traditions of the venerable Messenger; for example: "Die before you die," and "Human beings are asleep; they only wake up at death."

Taḥqīq is closed to all but those who are subject to the coercion of Allāh, who are endowed with a noble disposition, the spirit of abandon and genuine aptitude. The lot of other groups is imitation, consolation, and anticipation: marvelous tales and fables.

Vahdet'i vücûd (waḥdat al-wujūd [A]) (unicity of being: monism)
Tevhid (tawḥīd [A]) (affirmation of unity)
Unicity of Being—monism—is a primitive notion in the view of the Masters of Truth and Reality. It is a preparatory phase.

This is neatly expressed in the saying of the venerable Mevlânâ: "He is a fool [*aḥmaq*], who says that everything is God [*Ḥaqq*]."

The monistic view is common among theoretical seekers at the stage of gnostic wisdom. Salvation from this is possible only through rigorous spiritual training.

To say "I am the Truth" (*anā-lḤaqq*), whether in secret or openly, is not Sufism. It is illusion and error. This was not the way of the saints and intimates, elders and Masters. They have always aimed for the Unseen, non-existence, and ecstasy.

Vâhidiyyet (wāḥidiyya [A]) (uniqueness)
The quality of the Divinity at the level of "oneness of multiplicity" (*aḥadiyyat al-kathra*). Also called the "first individualization." This reality emerges with the experience of the annihilation of attributes. Above it lies Transcendent Unity (*aḥadiyyat al-'ain*).

Vecid (wajd [A]) (ecstasy)
The immersion of knowledge in insight.

The extinction of the potential in necessity. The obliteration of createdness in Divine Truth.

The annihilation in the Essence of laws, actions, names, and attributes.

The venerable Abū 'Alī al-Daqqāq said: "When Being departs, ecstasy remains."

Also known by such names as rapture, absence, the bewilderment of love, and so on.

Velâyet (walāya [A]) (sainthood)
Velâyet meşrebi (mashrab al-walāya [A]) (saintly disposition)
Sainthood is the state of one who has reached annihilation. It is superior to the level of prophecy. Some of the venerable Prophets have also been endowed with sainthood. But the informative or communicative function of prophecy always arises in every saint.

The "saintly disposition" is a satisfactory term to describe the novice's aptitude for annihilation and permanent non-being. It is the inclination to be weary of being and to contemplate the hereafter. Those who are endowed with this genuinely rapturous temperament are also said to be "subject to divine coercion."

The seeker who possesses this disposition will sooner or later achieve sainthood, that is, annihilation and permanent non-being, through steadfast striving on the path of Truth and Reality.

Vücûd (wujūd [A]) (being, existence)
The visible manifestation of non-existence.

Fixity, awareness, perception, knowledge.

The cosmos, the universe, perceptibles and intelligibles.

There is contingent being and there is real Being.

Contingent being is the universe of created things and phenomena.

Real Being is the Unseen, which is the extinction of the universe; it is non-existence, non-individualization.

Vücûdiyyât (wujūdiyyāt [A]) (existing beings)
Include everything in the universe that subsists in the senses, in the mind, and in knowledge. We are in this world of decline in proportion to our heedlessness. To the extent that we awaken and achieve annihilation, so do we progress in the world of Divinity by "annihilating the properties of Being."

Yakin (yaqīn [A]) (certainty)
The levels of Certainty are Knowledge of Certainty (*'ilm al-yaqīn*); Vision of Certainty (*'ain al-yaqīn*); Truth of Certainty (*ḥaqq al-yaqīn*).

These Certainties arise by mystical revelation and communion: Knowledge of Certainty at the annihilation of actions; Vision of Certainty at the annihilation of attributes; Truth of Certainty at the annihilation of Essence. They mark the attainment of the stages of Truth and creation.

Knowledge of Certainty marks the attainment of the spiritual world; Vision of Certainty marks the attainment of the world of real love; Truth of Certainty marks the attainment of the world of Essence. This process occurs gradually, as the properties of Being are removed, subjectively and objectively.

Yetim malı (māl al-yatīm [A]) (the orphan's property)
The state, station, and competence of the venerable Messenger, the Master by revelation and ecstatic experience of the degree of the Mystery of Ipseity. Also known as the extinction of individuality and the ultimate station. Attributed by proxy to the Cardinal of cardinals (*Quṭb al-aqṭāb*).

The beatitude of "as if it were not," achieved when the rest of existence is no more.

The spiritual quest is not completed as long as this point has not been reached.

Zât (dhāt [A]) (essence)
Zâtiyyet (dhātiyya [A]) (essentiality)
God's knowledge of Himself as an undifferentiated whole.

Above this lies the Mystery of the Mystery.

Essentiality means to be exempt from multiplicity and condescensions. It is the unmanifest. The state of perfect poverty and sound heart.

Dhātiyyāt (essentials) are the visions of annihilation and permanent nonbeing, the prospect of the world of Ipseity (*huwiyya*).

This degree is peculiar to those endowed with a disposition toward complete annihilation and extinction of individuality, the inheritors of the mantle of Muḥammad.

Bibliography

Primary Sources

***Nafaḥāt al-Uns min Ḥaḍarāt al-Quds* (Breaths of Divine Intimacy).** A Persian work by Mawlānā 'Abd al-Raḥman Jāmī, written in 881 of the Hijra at the request of Amīr Niẓām al-Dīn 'Alī Shīr Navā'ī. Translated into Ottoman Turkish by Lâmiî Chelebi of Bursa. Printed in Istanbul.

***Rashaḥāt-i 'Ain al-Ḥayāt* (Trickles from the Source of Life).** Written in Persian by Mawlānā 'Alī ibn Ḥusain Ṣafī. Translated into Turkish in 993 of the Hijra by Aḥmad Ra'ūf Chelebi. Printed in Istanbul in 1257 of the Hijra. A book of more than 400 pages.

Other Works Referenced

Jāmī. Persian work by 'Alī Aṣghar Ḥikmat. Printed in Tehran, 1340/1941. Turkish translation by M. Nuri Gençosman, Istanbul, Millî Basın Evi, 1949.

Maqāmāt-i Muḥammad Bahā' al-Dīn Naqshband. Persian work by Ṣalāḥ al-Dīn ibn Mubārak al-Bukharī. Turkish translation by Süleyman Azmi Chelebi in the reign of Sultan Mahmud I. Printed and published by Ali Kadri Bey. Also printed in Istanbul, Bahriye Press, 1328 of the Hijra.

Molla Jāmī. Turkish work by Âsaf Hâlet Chelebi. Printed in Istanbul, Kanaat Kitabevi, 1940.

***Risâle-i Bahâ'iyye* (*Risāla-i Bahā'iyya* in Turkish).** A Turkish work by Rıf'at Bey. Printed in Istanbul in 1306 of the Hijra. Written in two sections, each of which has five subsections. The first part deals with the basic teachings and methods of the Khwājagān and Naqshbandī Orders, while the second is a spiritual biography of Bahā' al-Dīn Naqshband. Written from the standpoint of monistic Sufism but contains some of the concepts of realization and verification.

***Thamarāt al-Fu'ād* (Fruits of the Heart).** Turkish work by Sarı Abdullah Efendi. Printed in Istanbul. A concise compendium of the main concepts of Islamic Sufism, its lines of transmission and important figures.

***Türk Edebiyyâtında Ilk Mütesavvifler* (First Mystics in Turkish Literature).** Turkish work by Professor Dr Fu'ad Köprülü. Printed in Istanbul, Âmire Press, 1918.